THE
PAPER
SHADE
BOOK

ROCKPORT

THE
PAPER
SHADE
BOOK

GLOUCESTER MASSACHUSETTS

ROCKPORT PUBLISHERS

Simple Techniques for Making Beautiful Lampshades

Maryellen Driscoll

First published in the United States of America by
Rockport Publishers, Inc.
33 Commercial Street
Gloucester, Massachusetts 01930-5089
Telephone: (978) 282-9590
Facsimile: (978) 283-2742
www.rockpub.com

ISBN 1-56496-753-0

10 9 8 7 6 5 4 3 2 1

Design: Terry Patton Rhoads
Cover Design: Cathy Kelley Graphic Design
Layout and Production: Cathy Kelley Graphic Design
Photography: Kevin Thomas Photography

The publisher gratefully acknowledges Barbara Mauriello's
Making Memory Boxes for "Tools" text.

Printed in China.

DEDICATION

To my 5th grade teacher Mrs. Cunningham, who, in between teaching me how to carry the zero in mathematics and encouraging me to memorize "Casey at the Bat," also taught me the basics of crafting. At the heart of crafting was her greatest lifelong lesson—making time for creative fun.

ACKNOWLEDGMENTS

Foremost, I wish to thank my editor, Shawna Mullen, who tolerated with the utmost grace my upside down schedule—fitting shades in between a summer of making hay, repairing the barn, butchering chickens, and traveling to New York to style food for national television. Her positive spirit never waned.

This book was also blessed by the hands-on talent of three gifted craft artists:

Katy McCabe, my niece and one of my best friends in life. She brought common sense, a fresh perspective, and her wry sense of humor to the workshop.

Livia McRee, my colleague and friend. She was the mastermind behind most of the fantastic votive projects in this book. Her quiet gift for crafting is sure to speak volumes in years to come.

Tara Millington, the penultimate cheerleader and ever-patient crafter. She came aboard early on in the book's process and was willing to do and redo anything until it was just perfect. She even cleaned the workshop when I stepped away for an afternoon. My gratitude outweighed my embarrassment.

I also want to thank Mary Ann Hall, a Rockport Publishers Acquisitions Editor, for steering me towards this book and offering me the most sage advice: "Keep it simple."

Finally, much thanks and boundless love goes out to my husband, Ken Fruehstorfer, who tolerated part of our house being strewn with papers, lamp bases, and fixtures for months on end. Often he let me off the hook from farm chores to work on this book. Sometimes I even managed to coordinate the two—measuring and cutting paper for shades on the hood of his truck (I did use a mat board) in between taking measurements and making cuts for him as he nailed in siding three stories up on our storm-broken barn. Whatever it takes.

CONTENTS

INTRODUCTION

A lampshade can be and should be much more than an unappreciated wallflower. It can act as an accent piece, soft-spoken and demure. It can punctuate its presence with elegant simplicity. Or it can step out as a bold statement, an intentional, unavoidable prop in a room's interior scenery. Just in its color alone a lampshade can influence whether a room feels warm or cool, subdued or vibrant.

A lampshade can reign in the harsh glare of a lit bulb without much—if any—attention to its size, color, or shape. It's the grim truth: a lampshade has the predestination to be drab.

However, hope for the neglected lampshade is anything but dim. What is beginning to transcend the long-forgotten shade is the arrival of a mind-boggling array of handmade and machine-made papers. You can readily find "paper" made from banana tree fibers, papyrus stems, or the hide of a goat. There are papers that look like crushed leather, wood grain, cloudy blue skies, cork facing. There are glorious wafer-thin lace papers, some with intricate patterns and others more organic, their patterns created by such elements as droplets of falling water. Many of these unique papers can be wrapped around or folded to make beautiful shades of all shapes and sizes. It can make night-lights, votive shades, and window covers, as well as lampshades. Light—be it from a basic bulb or candle's glow—becomes the perfect complement to paper's intricacies and marks of craftsmanship. With paper shades, the shade is not merely a means to insert light into darkness. The light, as well, comes to illuminate the shade and the awe-inspiring paper from which it is molded.

There's more good news: handmade and special machine-made papers can be remarkably affordable. With lampshade hardware being equally inexpensive, you can easily make your own lampshade, from some of the most gorgeous papers available, for under $20. Perhaps the most costly element to making a shade is your time, which all of the projects in this book set out to minimize by making the assembly as simple and straightforward as possible. Many projects are easily started and completed in an afternoon.

This book is divided into three categories: Traditional & Modern Shades, Exotic Shades, and Night-lights and Votives. So your choices are broad. Also, feel free to select a paper that best suits your personal taste. Each project offers general guidelines on the types of paper that will work with the shade. And most of the projects can be adjusted in size if you need to downsize or increase the size of the shade to better suit a lamp base.

CRAFTING TOOLS

Fortunately for the crafter, making lampshades does not require going out and purchasing a whole new array of tools. The basics will do. Listed on this page are most of the tools needed to complete the projects in this book. Not every tool shown here is required for every project. If any of the projects in this book require additional tools, they are listed in the specific project's materials list. For information on adhesives and glues see page 14.

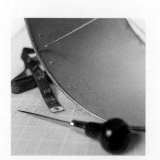

TOOLS

PENCIL
A pencil and pencil sharpener are important elements when measurements are being made.

KNIFE
Utility or mat knives, X-acto knives, or knives with snap-off blades are all acceptable and easily available at hardware and art supply stores. A surgical scalpel and good-quality curved blades can be purchased through bookbinding or surgical suppliers. A utility knife is best for cutting binder's board.

SCISSORS
Make sure they're good and sharp. Used mostly for rough cutting. Most accurate cutting is done with a knife and straight-edge or, for the best of all worlds, heavy-duty board shears.

RULER
A metal ruler or straight-edge is preferable to a plastic one that can be nicked or shaved when used with a knife. The heavier the ruler, the more secure the action. A cork backing prevents the ruler from sliding while cutting is being done.

SQUARE RULE
A square rule is used with a knife for cutting boards and other materials, and maintaining right angles. It is available at an art supply store.

LARGE MAT BOARD
A self-healing mat board, imprinted with a grid pattern, on which endless cuts can be made with your knives, are available in several sizes from bookbinding and art supply stores.

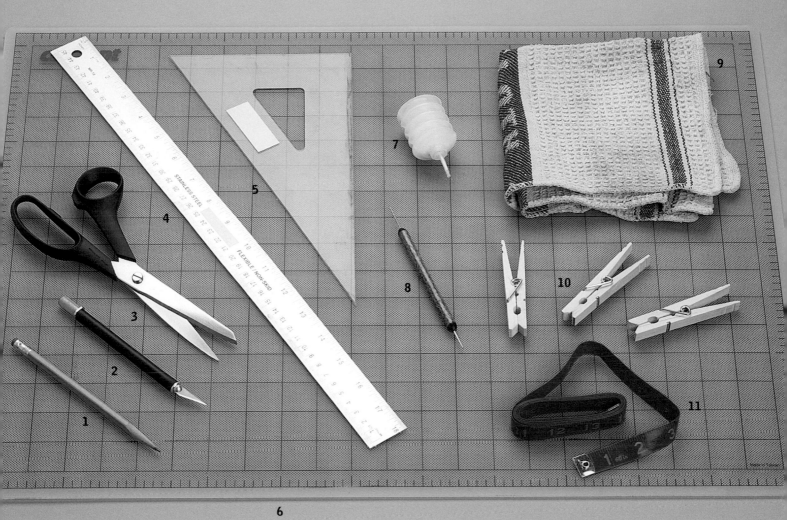

KEY

1. Pencil
2. Craft knife
3. Scissors
4. Ruler, preferably metal with a cork backing
5. Square rule
6. Large mat board
7. Glue dispenser with a long, narrow applicator

8. Awl
9. A damp rag for wiping away excess glue
10. Clothespins
11. Flexible seamstress measuring tape

GLUE DISPENSER
When choosing a glue dispenser, it's important to remember that a small hole lessens the potential for messy over-gluing.

AWL
A wooden-handled tool with a sharp, pointy metal shaft, used to punch holes. These are easily available at bookbinding suppliers and hardware stores.

DAMP RAG
Keep a damp cloth handy while gluing. Use it to clean

sticky fingers so that you do not get any unwanted glue on finished surfaces.

CLOTHESPINS
Use clothespins to hold pieces in place while glue is drying.

SEAMSTRESS TAPE
For circular shapes where measuring with a ruler would be awkward, seamstress tape is invaluable. It is widely available at craft stores and sewing shops.

FIXTURES AND FITTINGS

Before you begin to buy any supplies and fixtures for your lampshade, it is important to take a close look at the hardware on your lamp base to understand the kind of lampshade fixtures for which it is designed.

The majority of lamp bases are designed so that the shade sets on top of a harp and is bolted in place with a finial. In such cases, the appropriate top wire fixture on a lampshade is a washer top wire (also known as a spider top wire). A shade made with a washer top wire permits the greatest flexibility in terms of the type of shade you construct. It can basically be used with nearly all shapes and sizes of shades. It does, however, hinge on your having a harp from which to hang the shade.

If your lamp does not come with a harp, but you wish to make a shade using a washer top wire, most hardware stores carry various sized harps. They are easy enough to clip right on. If your lamp needs a harp wing, however, to hold the harp in place, you may have to detach the socket, which requires familiarity with how a lamp is wired. In this case you may consider using a bulb clip adapter.

FIXTURES AND FITTINGS

BULB CLIP TOP WIRE
A bulb clip top wire is easy to pop on and off. It requires no specific hardware on the lamp base other than a bulb to which it can clip. A bulb clip top wire, however, does not secure to the lamp as tightly as a washer top wire, so such top wires are best suited to smaller shades that are less likely to shift when clipped to a bulb. If you already have a top wire that is something other than a bulb clip, you may still readily convert it to a bulb clip by adding a bulb

clip shade adapter. If you wish, you can even purchase an adapter with a screw top to accommodate a finial. This comes in two styles: one for a standard bulb, the other for a flame-shaped bulb.

UNO TOP WIRE
This fixture actually props on the socket. Its inner circle is threaded so that it screws into place. Consequently, the lamp socket must also be threaded (known as a threaded uno socket) for the fixture to hold firmly in place. This style fix-

ture is most commonly paired with floor lamps.

BOTTOM WIRES
No matter which top wire you choose, the bottom wire is always simply a plain wire with no special attachments. Its job is to attach to the paper arc or other form that makes the shade. With some lampshade frames the bottom wires come connected to the top wires as a complete unit. The side wires that connect the two are called "ribs".

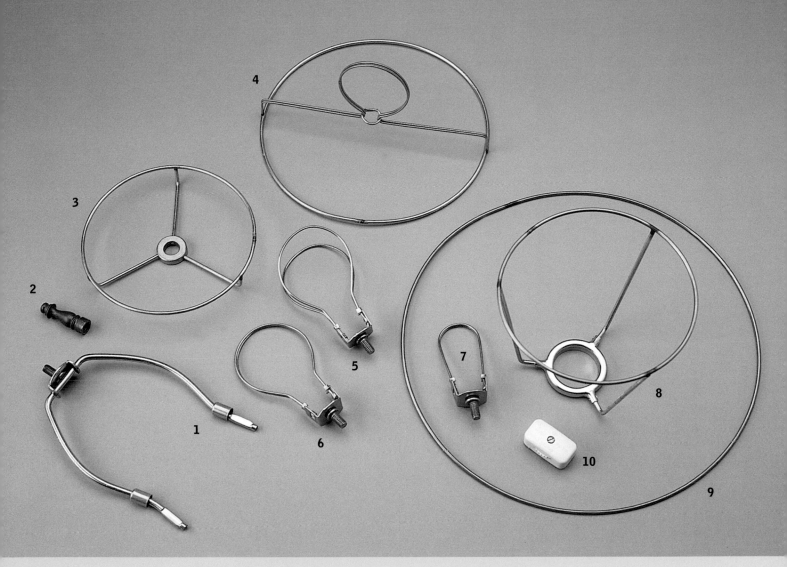

KEY

1. Harp
2. Finial
3. Washer top wire
4. Bulb Clip top wire
5. Bulb clip adapter
6. Bulb clip adapter with finial screw
7. Flame bulb clip adapter with finial
8. Uno top wire
9. Bottom wire
10. Cord switch

SHADE MEASUREMENTS
When ordering circular lampshade wires to make a drum-shaped, empire, or a cone-shaped shade, you will need the measurement of the shade's top and bottom diameter. That is the measurement that cuts across the center of the circular wire.

For most panel shades, be it a square, rectangular, or hexagonal shade, the shade frame comes in one unit. So you need the measurement of the top and bottom wires as well as the side wires for height. In the case of a rectangle, that means you need two sets of three measurements since there will be two different sized panels on the shade. The square coolie shade on page 62 and the woven rectangular shade on page 46 are examples of single unit frames. You can also find square-shaped top and bottom wires sold individually. The basic box shade on page 26 is constructed with separate top and bottom square-shaped wires.

CORD SWITCH
For some of the projects in this book, the shape or construction of the lampshade requires that the power switch on the lamp be located on the cord. If your lamp base switches on at the socket, you can alter this by installing a cord switch, also known as an in-line switch. You may find these switches at a hardware store. They come with straightforward instructions for installation.

GLUES & GLUING

Perhaps the most intricate process in making shades is the gluing. Imperfections common to gluing—rippling, buckling, blistering—will show and quickly diminish the visual effect of your shade. While it is important that you take your time when gluing or adhering papers to make shades, it is also important that you use the right adhesive. Following is a list of the basic glues and adhesives you will find used in this book, along with a description of their qualities and uses.

TIPS FOR APPLYING GLUES AND ADHESIVES

• When gluing a paper lining to a shade wire, apply the glue to the wire not to the paper.

• Make sure to spread a thin, even coat of glue. Ideally, use a glue applicator with a long, narrow tip for more precise application. Cotton swabs are handy when you need to spread any type of glue.

• When gluing paper to a shade wire, start at the center edge of the paper and work out. This is especially important with a round shade. (See Step 1 on page 22.)

• Place clothespins close together when first gluing paper to a lampshade wire. This is to help avoid gaps. Once the whole shade has adhered flat against the wire, remove every other clothespin to let the glue dry.

• When adhering with double-sided adhesive tape, first stick the tape to the liner or base paper in the project. Expose the second side by removing the protective cover in increments. This way you have a better chance of making corrections if the paper is not properly aligned.

PVA-POLYVINYL ACETATE

This is the ideal glue for adhering paper to lampshade wires. It is white but dries clear. It does not dry stiff but instead is almost rubbery in consistency. It does not disfigure paper or cause blisters. Also, it has a tack fast enough to grab the paper quickly but slowly enough to allow time for you to make adjustments. When applying PVA glue, it is ideal to use a narrow tipped glue applicator. (See Crafting Tools, page 10.)

DOUBLE-SIDED ADHESIVE TAPE

Double-sided adhesive tape, readily available in craft stores, can and will save you a tremendous amount of time and frustration when assembling shades. This clear plastic tape with "stick" on both sides is ideal for making flawless seams on shades as well as adhering paper over shade liners. This tape is also effective when working with thin or fragile papers or constructing the votive projects in this book. This product is commonly found in strip/tape form but also comes in sheets. For the projects in this book, make sure the tape is designed for a permanent seal.

SPRAY ADHESIVE

A couple of projects call for this adhesive. Be sure to cover your work surface with newspaper or other scrap paper when using the spray. Its airbound sticky particles travel. For a permanent bond, be sure to spray both sheets of paper that are to be glued together.

NEEDLE AND THREAD

In some projects here, the paper is not held to the shade with any glue or adhesive but, instead, with stitching. This technique is primarily used with delicate, fabric-like papers that are gathered or attached to shade wires without a lining.

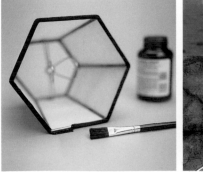

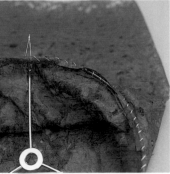

SURFACE EFFECTS

While you might start out with a flat sheet of paper, there are a wide variety of techniques you can apply to paper to create surface effects to your shade. These can enrich your shade with texture and add interesting play with shadows and light.

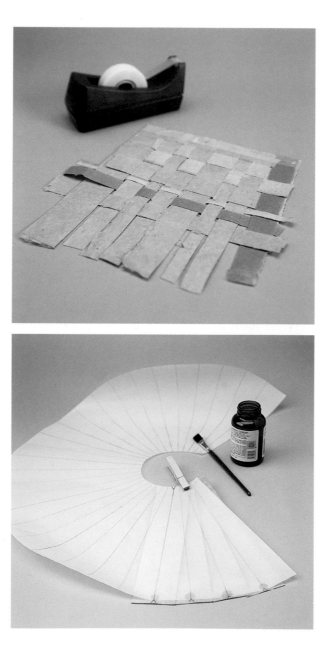

One way to change the surface of the paper is by manipulating it in some way. Crumpling, folding, gathering, overlapping, and fluting are all ways of creating varying effects. Weaving is another technique for creating surface texture.

Two other popular techniques for affecting the surface of a shade are cutting and piercing, both applied to projects found in the votive chapter starting on page 88. Cutting and piercing both offer a glimpse behind the shade, much like catching a peek inside a lit home. The effect is always intriguing. Placing these shades over the flicker of candlelight adds all the more visual enticement as the illuminated patterns dance against a dark wall.

You can easily experiment with both piercing and cut outs to formulate your own patterns and designs. Your designs can be geometric, abstract, or an outline of a favorite form or shape. You can also combine both techniques in creating your design.

It is always wise to place a protective covering over your work surface, such as a thick towel or a few layers of felt, when you are piercing paper. An awl (see Tools, page 10) is commonly used for piercing, but just about any sharp, pointed tool you can find will do. Various sized needles, an ice pick, or even a sharp nail would suffice. You can also play around with various sized piercings. Perhaps your largest might not even be a piercing at all but a circle created with a hole punch. Experiment.

With cutouts, it is easy to custom design your own pattern. The key is to avoid connecting lines in the paper. Similarly, when piercing, distance the holes by at least 1/8" to avoid breakage. It is best to create a template before cutting or piercing into the paper that is to be used for the finished shade. If the pattern is to be continuous around a shade, it is often a good idea to sketch a grid on the back of the paper you are working with as a guide for the pattern's even placement.

An effective finishing touch to pierced or cutout paper shades (or a flattering combination of both) is to back the shade with a contrasting translucent paper. This will help to enhance the design you've created and add an additional dimension of color to the shade.

THE BASE-ICS

When making a lampshade, there's no such question as "which came first: the chicken or the egg?" Before anything, you need to identify the base you are to use—unless you are making a hanging lamp. The good news is that a lot of the conventional rules for matching bases and lampshades have fallen by the wayside. So what you primarily need to do is to rely on your solid intuition, creative flair, and personal touch. Your lamp base and shade are meant to be an ensemble. It is almost like putting together an outfit. You will want both the components to complement one another—not to compete with each other for attention.

Dimensionally, the shade should reflect that of the base. Think balance. An itsy shade atop a hefty base is sure to look awkward. That is not to say, however, that you cannot try pushing the envelope. The idea is not necessarily to make the lamp invisible, camouflaged into the backdrop. It is to highlight its attributes and individuality. So while it is intuitive to coordinate a square base with a paneled shade, such as a square or rectangle, a drum shade could add an unexpected, pleasant flair.

Whatever shape or size you choose, do make sure your shade is long enough to cover the socket but not so long that it is hovering over the base. If you have either of these problems, one simple solution might be to change the size of your harp. A smaller harp will drop the shade; a larger one will give it life. If you are making a round empire shade and are uncertain about what length the sides of your shade should be, you can experiment by simply tying a few strings to suspend the bottom wire from the top.

ABOUT PAPER

Once you have decided on your lamp base, you can start to consider your paper—almost. Your first step in selecting a paper is to determine the function the lamp is to play in the room. Will the lamp be used for general lighting? Task lighting? Or will it simply function as an accent piece? The ramifications of your decision are two-fold. With your selected paper, you are creating a visual component—a shade—to the decorative landscape of a room.

Furthermore, that very shade will create a visual environment of its own by the manner in which it sheds light. Think about how far you wish your lamp to cast its light. Do you want the light to be focused or to splay across the room? Or maybe you want it to cast its light towards the ceiling. Also, what kind of feel do you wish the shade to create? Are you looking for warmth, or something modern and cool? It is the very paper from which the shade is constructed, not just the shape of the shade that creates an effect.

When selecting a paper, consider the paper's qualities—its strength, flexibility, and translucence. All can be crucial to the construction of your shade. For example, you don't want to make a gathered paper shade with a heavyweight, rigid paper. Rather, you need something soft and flexible, almost fabric-like. To optimize brightness, you will want to avoid a dark, opaque paper, which is more apt to create a somber atmosphere. Instead, choose a paper that is light and highly translucent. All of the projects in this book take these factors into account and offer suggestions for alternate papers if you cannot find the specific paper called for in the project.

As you are considering a particular paper for a shade, be sure to hold it up to the light. This helps you to gauge its translucency and also predict the characteristics of the paper that a light will enhance. Many papers take on a magnificently richer appearance when set before a light. Depending on your project, this may be desirable—or it may not. Similarly, feel the paper. Get a sense of its surface and substance. Many paper stores have binders filled with samples of their papers so that you are at liberty to touch them as much as you wish.

When shopping for your paper, be sure to bring a notepad with the measurements you need. If you can, also bring the lamp base. If in doubt, most paper stores will supply you with swatches at no cost. Take them home and consider your options. If you are ordering paper by mail, it is a particularly good idea to first request paper samples.

In addition to choosing a paper for the exterior of your shade, you will find that most of the shade projects in this book call for a lining. Heavyweight vellum or parchment papers are most often recommended since they are both translucent and sturdy in nature. The vellum does tend to be slightly more translucent and uniform. Parchment can be mottled but can also be easier to work with.

Finally, before making the ultimate commitment—cutting into the paper of choice—it is always good to make a mock-up of your shade with scrap paper. It helps you get acquainted with the shade-making process. It can also save you from making mistakes and wasting money on your prized paper of choice.

LAMPSHADE CRAFTING 101:
The Basic Shade

The round empire lampshade is the most basic of shades. Knowing how to make this classic is helpful in understanding many of the fundamentals behind making most any lampshade.

The following is a step-by-step outline of how to make a basic empire shade. Included are tips that will help you avoid potential problems in the process of crafting this and many other kinds of shades. Therefore, it is recommended that you read this section, and the following one on trims, before proceeding with any of the projects in this book.

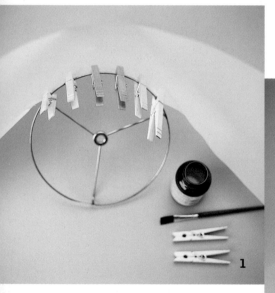

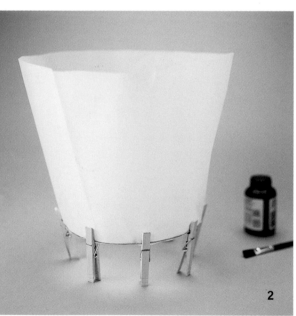

Step 1
Glue the arc-shaped lining paper, cut from a template, around the outside of the top wire. (See Templates page 110) Apply glue in a thin line, spreading evenly with a cotton swab if necessary. Start gluing at the center of the arc and work out, all the while securing it with clothespins placed close together to prevent the paper from shifting or gapping.

Tip: Unless specified, it is important with most paper shades to start out with a lining. Heavyweight vellum or parchment paper is most often recommended since they are both translucent and sturdy.

Step 2
Once the arc is attached to the top wire, remove every other clothespin and let dry.

Tip: Often the best way to prop the shade up so that it does not warp or shift while drying is to place it upside down so that it stands on the end tips of the clothespins.

4

3

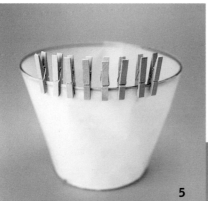

5

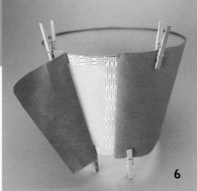

6

Step 3

Adhere the sides of the paper arc, which should overlap about 1/2", to form a seam. Double-sided adhesive tape is ideal.

Tip: Before sealing the seams, tape them together at the bottom of the shade first and insert the bottom wire to make sure it fits properly.

Step 4

If using glue to seal the seam, the following will insure that it dries without puckering. Sandwich the glued seam between 2 strips of foam package padding. Press the padding firmly against the seam by covering with two rulers or wooden slats held together with elastic bands.

Step 5

Set the shade upside down, and glue the bottom wire to the bottom of the shade. As in step 1, start from the center of the arc and place clothespins close together while attaching to prevent shifting and gaps. Once the shade is attached to the wire, remove every other clothespin and let dry.

Tip: Vellum tends to pucker as the glue dries. To smooth any rippling or puckering where the vellum has been glued to the frame wires, blow on it with hot air from a hairdryer. The heat will help to pull the paper taut.

Step 6

Apply double-sided tape or a line of glue around the top and bottom edges of the shade, as well as along the seam. Wrap around it the shade paper, which should have been cut into the same arc shape as the lining.

Now your shade is ready for the finishing touches.

Troubleshooting

- *In general, before cutting into the paper to construct your shade, you might make a mock-up with scrap paper and pin it up against your lampshade frame to make sure everything aligns properly. For any shade like the round empire shade that requires cutting the paper into an arc, it is better to cut the arc slightly larger (about 1/4 inch) than needed. In this way, you can comfortably fit the wires in place. If the paper hangs slightly over the wires, carefully trim away the excess with a craft knife.*

- *To make sure your top and bottom wires are perfectly parallel to one another, hold a ruler vertically against the shade and measure the length between the two wires all around the shade. It should be the exact same length all around. Otherwise, your shade will be lopsided. Do this before gluing the bottom wire; hold it in place with clothespins.*

- *You may wish to clip the paper to the shade with some clothespins to fit properly before adhering. Once wrapped snugly around the shade, unclip half of the paper and adhere to the liner. Repeat with the second half.*

TRIMMING LAMPSHADES

Besides giving a shade a clean, finished look, trim can be important in helping to hold the shade together. If you want to finish your shade with a traditional trim, it is important to make sure you select the correct type and size ribbon. Many ribbons, such as satin, will react negatively to glue and pucker and slide out of place. The ideal ribbon for trimming a paper shade is a ribbed ribbon known as grosgrain, which is made of a combination of 43 percent cotton and 57 percent rayon. Typically, those companies that sell lampshade fixtures also sell this particular trim in a wide assortment of colors and a variety of widths. To determine the size trim you need for your lampshade, measure how wide a trim outline you wish to have around the shade. Add that to the extra width you need to have the trim wrap over the frame wires and inside the shade. To measure the length of the trim, you need to measure the circumference of both the top and bottom of the shade. Use a flexible seamstress's tape to do so.

The following is a series of basic steps for applying trim. For hints on how to work with trim when applying to angled shades, see the trim steps for the hexagonal sconce shade on page 55.

1. Before applying the trim, use a ruler and pencil to mark where the edge of the trim should fall along the shade's top and bottom edges. This marking gives you a guide to follow when gluing on the trim so that it falls in a straight line. Allow the trim glued to the outside of the shade to dry before adhering the remainder to the inside.

   Tip: When gluing trim to a shade, apply a thin layer of glue to the trim, not to the shade, and do so in 3" intervals as you work around the shade.

2. Again, working in intervals, spread glue on the remaining trim and wrap it inside the shade, tucking it under the wires. Hold it in place with clothespins to dry.

3. When you run across the spokes of a frame's top wire, clip the ribbon to make a "V" so that the trim accommodates the spoke.

4. Always cut the ends of trim at a diagonal to prevent the ribbon from fraying. To complete the trim, glue the diagonal ends so that they overlap. When applying a narrow trim, such as the hemp cord here, finish by gluing the ends so that the tips meet.

5. Depending on the shade and the trim used (if any), you can also employ the end of the trim as an accent to the shade. Here the ends of the hemp cord were simply knotted together. Other ideas might be a button or a lightweight buckle.

BASIC BOX SHADE

The simple, clean lines of a box-shaped shade translate into a confidently understated form that needs few or no embellishments. For this project, a machine-made paper from Thailand known as unryu was used. This paper is made from mulberry pulp into which fiber strands are embedded. The effect is a lightweight, translucent paper that is ethereal yet deceptively strong. It seems fitting that unryu literally means "cloud dragon paper." This soft paper is not known for its folding properties, so it is wrapped around a stiff folded vellum box structure. This process ensures that the unryu fits snugly around the crisp corners of the shade.

The construction of this shade is straightforward. Instead of securing the paper to the wire framework with trim, the top and bottom edges of the paper fold at 90-degree angles toward the center to create a lidded effect. This serves two functions: it underscores the box feel without obstructing the passage of light, and it creates a structural flap so that the shade actually sits on the top frame wire, simplifying the construction.

Paper Choices

The options for paper are quite broad with this shade. The shape of the shade works best with a paper through which light can be emitted (otherwise, the light can seem too "boxed" in). The paper should also be able to make clean folded edges. Or, like the unryu, it should be supple enough that it can wrap snugly around the edges of the vellum so that there is still a crisp edge to the box shape.

Materials

- 1 strip of 25" x 7" (64 cm x 18 cm) plain, translucent vellum
- 1 strip of 25" x 7" (64 cm x 18 cm) orange unryu paper
- 1 square washer top wire, 6" x 6" (15 cm x 15 cm)
- 1 square bottom wire, 6" x 6" (15 cm x 15 cm)
- 1 finial
- Basic craft supplies (see page 10)

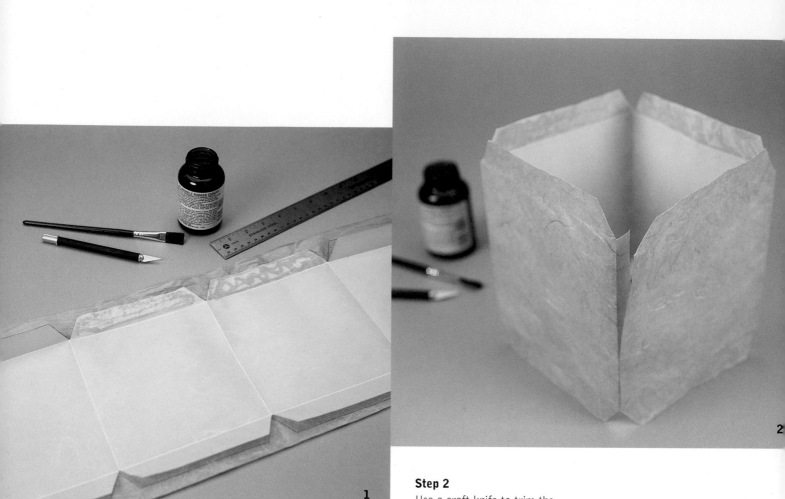

1

2

Step 1

Use the template on page 111 to cut the vellum. To make folds, use the blunt side of a craft knife to score the vellum where the dotted lines on the template are located. Fold along the scored lines in the same direction. Fit the folded vellum cutout over the unryu paper with the flaps folding away from the unryu paper (as shown). Using double-sided tape or a thin layer of glue, adhere the vellum to the unryu paper by its flaps starting with the top and bottom center flaps and working out. The four, 6" (15 cm) squares in the center of the vellum do not need to be glued to the unryu paper but should lie flat against it.

Tip: Vellum is likely to wrinkle when it comes in contact with glue. To minimize this effect, spread the glue onto the unryu paper, not the vellum. Use a light, even coat of glue. Let dry slightly, about 20 seconds, before adhering the vellum to the unryu paper.

Step 2

Use a craft knife to trim the unryu paper around the flap edges so that it fits flush with the edges of the vellum cutout. Apply double-sided tape or spread a thin, even layer of glue to the unryu paper along the inside (the vellum side) of the left side flap. Fold it over so that it sticks to the inside edge of the adjoining 6" (15 cm) vellum square. Run an even line of glue along the outside (the unryu side) of the right side flap. Bring the right side flap over to the glued left flap and adhere so that the unryu sides of the flaps are adhered together forming a box shape (as shown). Be sure the corners of the flaps are perfectly aligned for a nice square box shape. Secure with clothespins and let dry.

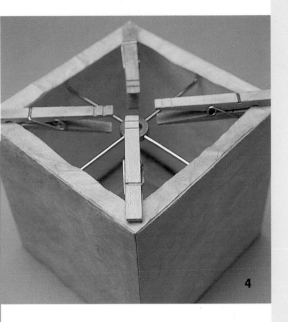

Troubleshooting

To make sure the lightweight bottom wire adheres snugly to the bottom flap edges as it dries in step 3, you may wish to set something on top of the wire as it dries. An easy solution is to place the top frame wire on top of the bottom wire. Then place something of weight, such as a can of beans, on top of the washer frame, where the finial would sit, to anchor the bottom wire onto the paper flap. The top frame wire may also need to be weighted down in a similar fashion.

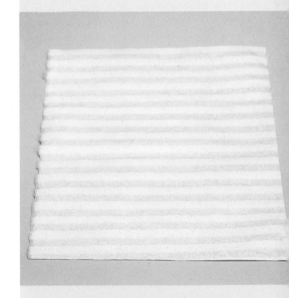

Step 3

Prop the box shape upright, folding the four, 1" (3 cm) wide bottom flaps under. Run a line of glue on the inside of these flaps along the crease line. Insert the bottom frame wire inside the box so that it sits on the lines of glue. Let dry. To glue the top wire, open the top flaps—so that the vellum side faces out—and run a line of glue along the crease line. Insert the top wire into the box. While holding the washer top wire in place inside the shade, fold the flaps back over so that the glue comes in contact with the wire. Carefully flip the box upside-down to let dry.

Step 4

To finish, glue the top flaps together where they overlap in the corners. Secure with clothespins and let dry. Then glue the bottom flaps in the same fashion.

Variation

Using a striped pattern for the box-shaped shade will make a bolder statement than the soft fibrous unryu. For a more finished appearance, you might wish to place trim around the folded edges or on the inside edges of the top and bottom flaps.

MODERN AND TRADITIONAL PAPER SHADES

PAPER TWIST CONE

This project uses readily available materials and supplies. The slender conical shade is decorated with everyday twisted craft paper, often used for bows on wreaths or floral arrangements. It is readily available at craft supply stores as well as at many general housewares stores. A liquid laminate will give the shade a glossy finish—a modern, vinyl-wrapped look. The tall, narrow shape of this shade makes it a perfect choice for a table where space is limited. Its lack of transparency makes it best suited as an accent lamp. This way the light bulb sits lower and at a safe distance from the sides of the shade. Be sure to use a tapered light bulb, such as those shaped like a torch flame.

Materials

- 1 sheet of 14" x 20" (36 cm x 51 cm) dark, rigid paper or poster board (navy or black)

- 1 string of 6" (15 cm) marine blue twisted craft paper

- 1 string of 16" (41 cm) marine blue twisted craft paper

- 1 string of 20" (51 cm) marine blue twisted craft paper

- 1 string of 22" (56 cm) marine blue twisted craft paper

- 1 string of 15" (38 cm) marine blue twisted craft paper

- 1 washer top wire, 4" (10 cm)

- Liquid laminate

- Basic craft supplies (see page 10)

1

2

Step 1

Unravel the measured twisted craft paper strings loosely, flattening them without pressing out the fine creases. The strings should unravel to a width of 2 ½" to 3" (6 cm to 8 cm).

Step 2

Use the template on page 112-113 to cut the dark paper or poster board into a cone shape. Glue the unraveled paper strips to the cone at a diagonal. Begin by gluing the 22" (56 cm) strip. Its lower left edge should sit at the lower left corner of the cutout. Its upper right edge should lay 2" (5 cm) below the upper right hand corner of the cutout (as shown). Lay the remaining strips at the same angle. The strips should be placed from the top right hand corner to the lower left hand corner in the same order listed above under "Materials." All of the strips hang over the cutout's edge by at least ½" (1 cm).

Step 3

Trim the glued strips so that there is a ½" (1 cm) overhang, except on one of the straight edges, where you should trim the strips flush to the straight edge.

Tip: Because of the creases in the twisted paper, you may find it easier to use scissors instead of a craft knife when trimming the untwisted strips of paper.

Troubleshooting

*This shade is designed to be rigid
since the frame sits in the center of
the shade and does not provide much
structure. If you are using poster
board to make a rigid cone, it may be
too stiff to hold in a cone shape to
glue the seams together in step 5. If
so, let the shade acclimate to the
shape overnight. Roll the shade into
its cone shape. Hold the ends of the
cone into shape by clipping the seam
ends with small spring-loaded binder
clips. Place a good padding of paper
towel or tissue paper in between the
clips and the shade so that they do
not leave an imprint in the paper. Tie
3 strings about 2" (5 cm) apart around
the center of the cone to cinch it in
place. Let the shade sit overnight in
the cone shape. To glue the seams
together, remove the spring-loaded
clips but not the strings. Work around
the strings, which help to hold the
cone shape in place as the glue dries.*

Step 4
Along the top curved edge of
the cutout, make slits every ½"
(1 cm) along the overhanging
marine strips, cutting to the
cone edge. Do the same along
the bottom curve at 1" (3 cm)
intervals. Glue the overhanging
marine strips along the 3 edges
to the cutout.

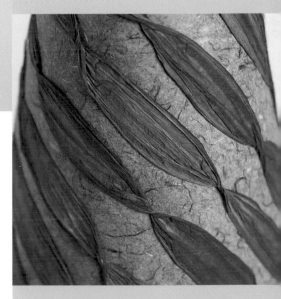

Step 5
Shape the cutout into a cone
shape overlapping the straight
edges by ½." Glue the overlapping straight edges together,
placing the edge with the marine
paper folded over it on the outside (see troubleshooting). Let
dry. Coat the outer edge of the
wire frame with glue and place
inside the cone as deep as it
will fit (about 3" (8 cm) from
the very top). Be sure it is set
straight in the cone; otherwise,
the shade will sit on the lamp
lopsided.

Variation

*Indulge in a bit of creativity by
experimenting with the concept of
using twisted craft paper to decorate
lampshades. For example, instead of
untwisting an entire strand, in this
variation the paper was unraveled
only at intervals.*

FLUTED DRUM SHADE

When patterned paper is fluted, a certain degree of intrigue is created as the pattern travels in and out of the shadows of the shade's curves. Linear prints are particularly effective with this style of shade. Here a gold print was used to complement the base. A thin gold soutache trim follows the wavy paper edges to give the shade a more finished look. For a more modern look you might use a less controlled patterned paper or you could reverse the approach. That is, use a bold patterned paper for the shade lining instead of the solid green used in this project. Then use transparent vellum for the fluting. Whichever approach you take, the key to making a fluted shade is being compulsive about accuracy. The design is easily adjusted to varying sizes of drum-shaped shades as well as to the width of the paper's flute. To do so, see instructions in "Size Variations" on page 39.

Paper Choices

Knowing the size of the flute is key when selecting a paper for any fluted shade. Knowing the size, you can test whether the paper can comfortably be fluted. For any fluted shade, a paper of medium weight is key. It must be supple enough to bend with the curves without buckling, yet it must be sturdy enough to hold its form without sagging.

Materials

- 1 sheet of transparent vellum, cut into a 7 ½" x 26" (19 cm x 66 cm) rectangle

- 1 sheet of 8 ½" x 26" (22 cm x 66 cm) medium green unryu paper (or other background paper)

- 1 sheet of 7 ½" x 40" (19 cm x 102 cm) India Woodblock paper (or other patterned paper of soft, medium construction weight*)

- 8" (20 cm) top lampshade wire

- 8" (20 cm) bottom lampshade wire

- 2 yards (1.8 m) plus 1 foot (.3 m) of ⅛"-inch (.3 cm) gold trim

- Basic Craft Supplies (see page 10)

*If you cannot find a sheet of paper 40 inches long (102 cm), then glue two sheets together. However, be sure that the overlapping seam falls on the inside curve of the fluting flush against the shade lining. (See step 4.)

1

2

Step 1

Run a line of glue around the top shade wire and attach a long edge of the vellum sheet. Use clothespins to hold it in place as the glue dries. Before gluing the seam, fit the bottom wire, holding it snuggly in place with clothespins. This way you will know if the seam needs minor adjustment. Adhere the seam using double-stick tape or glue. If gluing, let dry. Then, as with the top wire, glue the bottom wire to the opposite long edge of the vellum sheet to form a drum.

Step 2

Lay the green paper flat on your work surface. Pencil in the following grid as a guide for the fluting placement: 1" (3 cm) below the top, long edge of the paper and 1 ¼" (3.5 cm) in from the left edge pencil in a 5" (13 cm) vertical line. Repeat across the paper, spacing the lines 1 ¼" (3.5 cm) apart. Or, if your paper is too dark for the pencil to show through, use a white colored pencil or fabric pencil.

Step 3

Wrap the green paper around the drum with the grid facing out, allowing a ½" (1 cm) overlap on the top and bottom edges. Run a line of glue along the inside edge of the top wire and about ¼" (.5 cm) beneath it as well. Pull the green paper snuggly over the glue-coated top wire and press against the inside edge of the vellum drum where the second line of glue was run. Press down so that the paper is flush against the wire and drum interior. Repeat the gluing process at the bottom of the shade clipping with clothespins to hold in place if necessary.

Step 4

Place the patterned paper flat on your work surface with its patterned side (front side) facing down. On the backside, draw a 7 ½" (19 cm) vertical line down the paper, two inches (5 cm) to the right of the left short side of the paper. Repeat across the paper, spacing the lines 2" (5 cm) apart. Make a gentle fold along each penciled line, folding so that the front side of the paper is on the inside of the fold.

Step 5

With the patterned side of the paper facing out, align a seam edge of the patterned paper with the seam edge of the green paper drum. Run a thin line of glue along the green paper's seam edge and cover with the edge of the patterned paper. Clip in place with clothespins to dry. Next to the seam in the direction in which the patterned paper is wrapping, run a thin line of glue along the penciled vertical line drawn on the green paper.

Align the first fold line of the patterned paper with the line of glue on the green paper to form the first flute. Clip to the side of the flute to hold it in place as it dries. Continue gluing the fold lines every 1 ¼" (3.5 cm) along the drum's circumference until you have fully worked around the shade. Finish by gluing the gold trim around the top and bottom edges of the fluted shade.

To make the fluted drum style with a different sized shade and/or a different width of fluting, make a "dummy" with scrap paper before proceeding. Avoid gluing by using standard invisible tape to adhere the paper to the frame at the top and bottom edges. Place the finished dummy shade on the lampshade base to view. Because the fluting can dramatically enlarge the circumference of the drum, adjust the fluting size or the drum size so that the shade is in balance with the base.

Variation

To adjust the flute size, measure the width of the flute you wish to form. That is, make a sample curve of the paper and measure the distance between the beginning and end of the curve. Wrap a flexible seamstress's measuring tape around the top or bottom drum edge to measure its circumference. Divide the drum's circumference by the width of the flute to determine if it is an even fit, bearing in mind that the end of the last flute will overlap with the beginning of the first at the seam. The resulting figure should be a whole number.

JAPANESE TABLE LANTERN

The simple appeal of a Japanese-styled lantern can add a clean, modern look to a bedroom or dining table. Elegant Japanese rice paper is relatively easy to work with, score, and cut. Rice papers vary in texture depending on the materials added in the making: wood shavings, bark, flower petals, and strands of cotton or wool. If you wish to choose a different kind of paper, keep in mind the effect it will have on the light. Thin translucent papers create a luminous lamp. Textures in such papers add a decorous, natural feel to the lantern, and to the room that it's in. For a more traditional look, arrange the wood panes so that they divide the panels evenly, like a window.

Materials

- Balsa or basswood strips: four ½" wide (1 cm) strips, and four ¼" wide (.5 cm) strips (these are available at hobby and craft stores and come in approximately 24" long 61 cm strips)

- Thin piece of plywood, no less than ⅛" (.3 cm) thick but no more than ¼" (.5cm) (small pieces are also are available at hobby and craft stores)

- Thin, handmade rice paper

- White cardstock

- Light-colored wood stain and finish-in-one

- Hobby saw attachment for craft knives

- Basic craft supplies (see page 10)

Step 1
From the ½" wide (1 cm) strips, cut eight 12" long (30 cm) strips. From the ¼" wide (.5 cm) strips, cut eight 5" (13 cm) strips, eight 2 ⅜" (6 cm) strips, and four 9 ½" (24 cm) strips using the hobby saw. Cut the plywood to be 6" (15 cm) square. Cut the rice paper into four pieces measuring 6" wide by 10" tall (15 cm x 25 cm). Make sure that each piece is exactly the same size, and properly squared up.

Step 2
Sand the pieces of wood to their appropriate lengths, if needed. Also sand off any splinters in the wood. One the ½" (1 cm) wide pieces, be sure that the ends are level with each other so that the lantern will be steady. Using a foam brush, apply the stain according to the manufacturer's directions.

Step 3
Make reinforcements for the corners of the lantern: cut four ½" wide by 9 ⅞" (1 cm x 25 cm) long strips from the white cardstock. Lightly score them with the craft knife down the center of the length. Fold the paper to make a 90-degree angle. From the rice paper, also cut four ½" wide by 9 ⅞" long (1 cm x 25 cm) strips and glue them into the corner. They do not need to be scored because the paper folds easily.

Also make reinforcements for the inside bottom of the lantern where the panels meet the base of the lantern. Repeating the above technique; make four more reinforcements 5 ⅞" long (15 cm).

Step 4

To assemble each panel, glue a ½" wide (1 cm) piece of wood flush with a long edge of the paper, so that the stick extends 1" (3 cm) to the paper above and below. Repeat with the other long side.

Step 5

Once all the panels have dried, glue one at a time to the 6" (15 cm) square base, aligning the bottom edge of each panel with the bottom edge of the paper. Wait for the glue to set, but not dry completely before going on to the adjacent side. When you create a corner, glue a reinforcement into the corner to keep the lantern together and squared as you go. Finally, add the smaller reinforcements where the paper sides meet the base.

COFFEE-DYED LAMPSHADE
with Copper Lashing

Crumpling soft, Koji paper creates a shade with an organic elegance. Staining it in coffee lends an additional vintage feel. By lashing the soft, cylindrical shape with copper, the shade is pulled together both literally and figuratively. The effect is an hourglass-shape table lamp that channels light upwards and downwards, and defines space as it accents a room. The upward dispersal of light helps to further draw the viewer's attention to this lovely piece.

To make this shade you need a "slip uno frame" (see page 12 for more). The upside-down cone shape of the frame will fit snugly on the lamp socket. Two cones made from stiff vellum are joined at their smallest ends to form an hourglass shape: They basically hang from the uno frame and provide a framework for the soft crumpled paper to fit around.

__Important note:__ The unusual shape of this shade makes it difficult to reach the socket to switch the light off. If the lamp base you are working with does not have a cord switch, you can buy a cord switch at your local hardware store and easily install it yourself. (See Fixtures and Fittings, p. 12)

Paper Choices

This shade calls for paper that is supple enough to be crumpled without marked resistance—but strong enough to stand on its own (without framing or structural wires) after it is crumpled and shaped into a cylinder. If you choose to dye the paper, you must also be certain that it is absorbent. Koji, a native paper of Japan, is an ideal choice. To create a more daring look, another option would be a foil-type paper.

Materials

- one large pot of strong, warm coffee
- two old bath towels
- two medium-size elastic bands
- two 16" x 22" (41 cm x 56 cm) sheets of Koji paper
- two 12" x 19" (30 cm x 48 cm) sheets of stiff, translucent vellum
- one 5" x 4 1/2" (13 cm x 11 cm) slip uno lampshade frame
- 30" (76 cm) string
- 34" (86 cm) copper wire
- Basic craft supplies (see page 10)

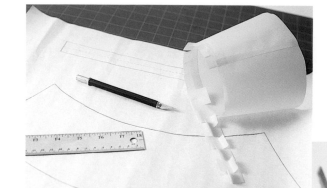

3

1

Step 1

Crumple each sheet of koji paper into a relatively tight ball. Secure each ball with two rubber bands to hold in place. Pour the warm coffee into a medium heat-proof bowl or saucepan. Submerge the paper balls in the coffee and let sit for about one hour so that they become fully saturated. For an even darker shade, let sit an additional hour or more.

2

Step 2

Remove the balls from the coffee and gently unravel, taking care not to tear the paper. Loosely spread each sheet out flat on a towel to dry. Don't smooth the paper too much, since part of the effect is the way the dye collects and dries in the creases. Be sure to use towels that you use around the house for rags since the coffee will stain them.

Step 3

Use the templates on page 114 to cut out two cones and a long narrow "collar" strip from the vellum. Score the center of the collar strip with a craft knife, using the dotted line as a guide. Next, make slits about $1/2"$ (1 cm) apart from the score to the long edge of the collar. Repeat on the other side, staggering the slits to make "flags," as shown above. Glue the sides of each cone template to form two equal-sized cones $1/2"$ (1 cm) overlap at seam. Then glue the short ends of the collar strip together $1/2"$ (1 cm) overlap to form a band.

Step 4

Create an hourglass shape with the cones by gluing the top half of the band to the in-side of the cone at its smallest opening (bend back the slit "flags" so that they adhere to the cone's interior). Once dry, glue the bottom half of the band to the small opening of the second cone in the same manner. Brush glue on the top and side wires of the uno frame and slip it into one of the cones, as shown. Clip around the edge of the cone to hold the frame flush against it while the glue dries.

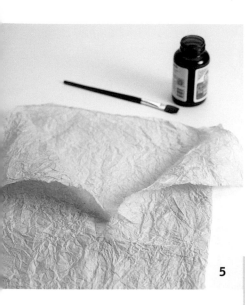

5

Step 5
Taking a sheet of the stained, crumpled paper, overlap the 16" (41 cm) edges by 1/2" (1 cm) and glue together to form a cylinder. Repeat with the second sheet of paper. Allow both to dry thoroughly, then slip one inside the other. For this shade, a light, relatively smooth koji was selected. Its weight and texture are easy to work with, and would be best likened to that of cotton tissue paper or a sheet of fabric softener.

6

Step 6
Set the hourglass cone on top of the lamp socket so the uno frame is on the top half. Slip the double-layered cylinder over the cone. Making sure it's centered, grasp the paper cylinder at the "waistline" of the hourglass and secure with string. Adjust the cinched crumpled cylinder so it gathers and softly flares. Wrap the copper wire around the "waistline" and twist a few times. Curl each of the wire ends in to make small loops.

Variation
Try fabric dye for a brighter color range. For a uniform beige tone, soak the paper in coffee without crumpling it first, smooth flat to dry. Instead of coffee, stain absorbent paper with tea, the juice of crushed berries, beet juice, or fabric dye. Test your dye source on a small swatch of your paper. Another variation is to twist the paper instead of crumpling it to get creases that run vertically along the shade, as was done with both of these pieces. Here, the solid colored swatch was dipped in the dye first and then twisted for an even coloring. The mottled "tie-dye" effect of the second swatch was created by twisting the paper, securing it so it did not unravel, and then soaking it briefly in the dye so it did not become fully saturated.

BASKET WEAVE

Crafting this shade can carry you back to grade-school days of weaving paper simply for the amazement of it—or for crafting paper Easter baskets for the joy of it. You can take a wide variety of approaches with this shade. For example, you can tear the strips for a more natural look; or cut them with a craft knife for more precise, clean lines. You can cut strips of even width for uniformity in the weave; or vary them for a slightly more modern, personal touch. The look of the shade is equally as affected by the color scheme as by the weave pattern, i.e. how you place the different colored paper strips in the weave. Feel free to play with this shade. It easily adapts to a square frame. It also can be made to wrap around a drum-shaped shade. A round or empire shade is the one basic form that does not translate easily to a basic weave.

Materials

- 1 rectangular lampshade frame 12" x 10" x 8" (30cm x 25cm x 20cm) and 7" x 5" x 8" (17.5cm x 13cm x 20cm): (measurements indicate length of bottom wire by length of top wire by height)

- 1 sheet of 20" x 30" (50cm x 75cm) neutral colored vellum or parchment

- 1 sheet of 20" x 30" (50cm x 75cm) dark sand-colored handmade paper

- 1 sheet of 20" x 30" (50cm x 75cm) pale peach handmade paper

- 1 sheet of 20" x 30" (50cm x 75cm) pumpkin-colored handmade paper

- 3 yards (2.7m) of ½" (1 cm) wide sand-colored paper trim

- Scrap paper

- Adhesive tape

- Basic craft supplies (see page 10)

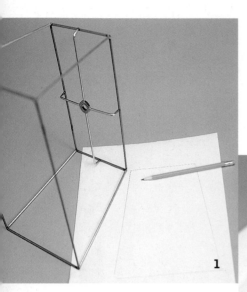

1

2

Step 1

Trace each side of the frame onto the neutral colored paper. Cut out each tracing and glue it to the wire frame to create a backing for the woven shade.

Step 2

On a scrap piece of paper, trace one of the long and one of the short sides of the frame. Using pencil and ruler, draw a mock grid of how you wish the woven pattern to look. You can go with varied sized strips for a contemporary look or strips of the same width for a more traditional basket weave. Mark the width of the strips needed along the side of the grid.

Step 3

Tear vertical strips from the four different colored hand-made papers according to the grid you designed. There is no prescription for how many strips of a particular color need to be cut. This is up to you. For example, if you wish the shade to take on a stronger peach/pumpkin tone, tear more strips of those colors. Align the vertical strips next to each other on a piece of scrap paper and secure in place at the top with tape.

4

Troubleshooting

Before gluing the frame to a woven swatch, make sure the weave is square. That is, make sure the vertical and horizontal strips are intersecting at 90-degree angles. Also, adjust large gaps between strips. Slight gaps, however, can make for a nice effect when the bulb is lit and slits of light shine through.

Step 4

Tear the horizontal strips of paper according to the grid To weave, start with the top horizontal strip and run it over and under the vertical strips. Continue down the grid, alternating between "over" and "under" for the starting point of each horizontal piece.

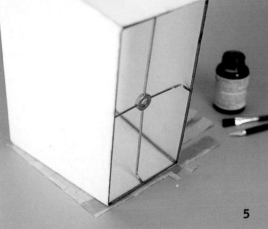

5

Step 5

Lay the frame over the woven pattern making sure it is square with the weave, i.e. the edges of the top and bottom horizontal strips are in line with the top and bottom frame wires. Glue around the frame edge and set the frame on top of the woven pattern to adhere. Once dry, trim away the portion of the weave that hangs over the frame edge. Repeat, gluing weave to the other three sides of the frame and trimming away the excess. Once complete, apply sand-colored trim around the top and bottom edges of the shade, as well as down the side corners. This trim should only run on the shade front; it is apt to split if folded over the wire framework.

Variation

Instead of tearing strips of paper, save time by weaving strips of paper ribbon.

PUNCHED PAPER STRING LIGHTS

String lights, so essential for a festive mood during the holidays, can be fun any time of the year and may be just the thing to liven up a theme party. Medium-weight papers will hold their shape when folded but are still thin enough to let light shine through. Create your own designs using specialty punches and deckle scissors. Choose colors and shapes to fit the desired mood. Papers in greens and blues will give off a more subdued, calming light than the festive colors shown here. More or larger cutouts will increase the light also altering the effect. For a softer light through the punches, line your shades with white or colored vellum.

Materials

- String lights
- Star and sun paper punches
- Three large sheets (about 19" x 25" (48 cm x 64 cm) of medium-weight art paper, such as pastel paper, of the following colors: red, yellow, and orange
- Double-sided tape
- Deckle edge paper edgers
- Basic craft supplies (see page 10)

Step 1

From one of the colors, cut out four panels measuring 6" x 12 ½" wide (15 cm x 32 cm). From each of the other two colors, measure and cut three panels of the same size.

Step 2

Measure up 2 ½" (6 cm) from one of the panel's long edges, and draw a line from short edge to short edge; then mark a line 1 ¾"(4.5 cm) up from the same edge. Place the ruler on the 2 ½"(6 cm) mark and fold the paper up along it. Then remove the ruler and make a sharper fold. Do not fold along the other line. Repeat for all the panels of paper.

Next, fold each panel into fifths, using the ruler and technique described above; each section should be 2 ½" wide (6 cm). Make each fold in the same direction to form the shade.

Make flaps for the shade by cutting along the creases that have divided the shade into fifths, starting at the longer edge of the paper where you measured up 2 ½" (6 cm) to begin with, and stopping once you get to the horizontal fold. Using the previously marked line 1 ¾" (4.5 cm) from the edge of the paper that you didn't fold as a guide, trim the first, third, and fifth flaps; they should measure ¾" (2 cm).

Punch a random design in the second, third, and fourth sections at this point.

Step 3

Bring the first and last panels together and align them. Secure with double-sided tape rather than glue to avoid warping the shades. Punch the fourth side of each shade. Then, gently flatten each shade and trim the edge with the deckle-edge scissors.

Step 4

Place a light in between the short flaps of one of the shades, then fold the two longer flaps over the string and each other; secure with double-sided tape.

Tip: Make a sample lantern and see if you like the size in relation to your light string. Some string lights may have close-together lights that will look better with smaller shades; simply reduce the panel height and width proportionately to make a smaller shade.

HEXAGONAL SCONCE SHADE

Capping a sconce lamp fixture with a hexagonal shade adds an elegant touch to the wall of any room or hallway. This shade is designed to fit over a narrow flame-shaped bulb. For a larger lampshade, follow the same instructions for this project, but adjust the measurements of the paper and trim accordingly. The same general instructions can also be easily applied to making "paneled" shades of other shapes.

Contrasting trim on a panel shade will provide a sharp border. If you wish to avoid this look, choose a trim that is closer to the color of the shade. Always use a narrower trim down the side wires of the lampshade frame than that along the top and bottom wires.

Materials

- 1 sheet of 20" x 25 ½" (50 cm x 65 cm) white crinkled paper

- 1 large sheet or 6 sheets of 8 ½" x 11" (22 cm x 28 cm) white vellum

- 3 feet (2.7 m) of ⅜" (1 cm) black grosgrain trim

- 3 feet (2.7 m) of ⅜" (.5 cm) silver soutache trim

- 1 clip hex frame, 4" x 6" x 5" (10 cm x 15 cm x 13 cm), for a flame-style bulb

- Wooden clothespins

- Basic craft supplies (see page 10)

Step 1

On a scrap piece of paper, outline one side of the shade to make a template. Use the template to cut out 6 vellum panels. (See Troubleshooting and page 115.) Use the same template to cut out six panels of the crinkled paper.

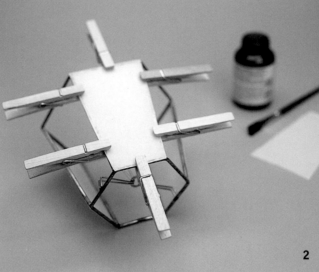

Step 2

Apply a thin line of glue along the wires surrounding one panel of the frame. Center one of the six vellum cutouts over the panel wires. Beginning at the center and working out, use clothespins to clip the paper first to the top and then to the bottom wires. Next, clip along the sides. Apply two more panels to the frame as instructed above, leaving an open panel between each pair. At this point, you will have covered every other panel on the frame. Allow the glue to dry thoroughly.

Step 3

Glue the remaining three vellum cutouts to the frame. You will only be able to clip along the top and bottom wires. Run your finger down the sides of each panel to insure the vellum makes contact with the glue. Once dry, adhere one of the six crinkled paper cutouts to each panel of the shade using double-sided adhesive tape or glue.

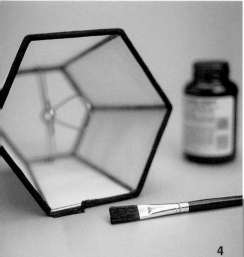

4

Step 4

Apply the black trim along the
outside bottom of the shade,
wrapping it over the wire
towards the inside of the shade.
You will need to miter the trim
at each corner to make it lie
flat. Repeat process to apply
trim to the top wire. Let dry.

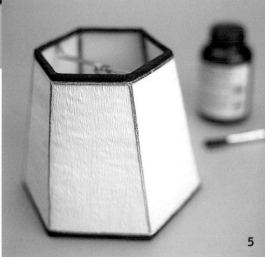

5

Step 5

Glue the silver soutache
along the bottom edge
of the top trim and to
the top edge of the
bottom trim. Glue the
remaining soutache
down the side wires of
the frame to cover the
seam between the six
adjoining panels.

Variation

*For a softer look, trim the shade
with torn strips of medium green
paper. The irregular edges and wider
bands of trim create a more casual
look. Choose a pliable paper for
trim so that it will easily conform
to the angles of the shade.*

LACED NAUTICAL SHADE

This is a bare minimum shade with clean lines and few fixtures. Yet the shade is as much decorative as it is functional, with brass grommets and hemp lacing contributing to an open, nautical look. Although this shade was designed for a hanging lamp, it can easily be adjusted to sit on a lamp base.

While a variety of papers could be used to make this shade, simple papers work best. Here, a white parchment paper with subtle mottling was chosen, as it mimics the burlap-like fabric of a ship's sail. Just as important is the paper you use to back the shade. This shade hangs without any structural wiring, so the shade must be backed with a sturdy paper to provide support. It should not be so stiff, however, that it cannot comfortably wrap into a loose, drum-like shape.

Materials

- 1 large sheet of lightweight white parchment cut into a 36" x 11" (91 cm x 28 cm) rectangle
- 1 large sheet of heavyweight white parchment or vellum cut into a 36" x 9" (91 cm x 23 cm) rectangle
- Double-stick adhesive tape
- 20 brass grommets
- Inserting grommet handle
- Hammer
- Towel or thick felt
- 5 ½ feet (1.7 m) of hemp string
- 1 bottom lampshade wire, 12" (30 cm) in diameter
- 13 feet (4 m) of brass wire (28 or 24 gauge)
- 1 brass ring
- Basic craft supplies (see page 10)

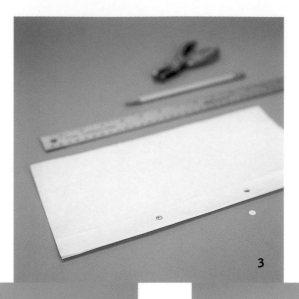

Step 1

On the lightweight parchment, use the back edge (the blunt edge) of a craft knife to score fold lines (top and bottom) parallel to and 1" (3 cm) in from the long edges of the paper. Fold the top and bottom 1" (3 cm) flaps over to the same side of the paper. This will be the front side of the shade.

Step 2

Adhere the stiffer, heavyweight parchment to the backside of the folded parchment, using double-stick adhesive tape. Be sure the folded side faces out. If your heavyweight parchment tends to curve (from being rolled) making it difficult for the paper to adhere, attach paper clips along the edge to hold the papers together. (Once the grommets are in place, it is less important that the two papers adhere.)

Step 3

Use a punch to puncture holes set 3 ¾" (10 cm) apart along the center of the folded bands. Start the first hole 1" (3 cm) in from the far left edge so that you do not end up positioning a grommet where the seam falls.

Step 4

Place a grommet through the front of the shade so that the post sticks out the back. Place the flat, washer-like piece over the grommet post on the backside of the shade. Place an inserting grommet handle into the post and strike with a hammer to seal. Make sure you lay a towel or piece of thick felt between the paper and your work surface before hammering.

5

6

Step 5

Overlap the opposing short edges of the paper by ½" (.5 cm) and glue to create a cylinder shape. Loop hemp string through the holes and over the wire ring to hang the shade. (See Troubleshooting.)

Step 6

Thread a 34" (86 cm) brass wire through the brass loop, folding the wire in half where it passes through the loop. Bend the wire ends under the lampshade wire and then twist the wire around itself to hold it in place. Use wire cutters or sturdy scissors to clip any extra.

Tip: To adjust this shade so that it sits on a lamp base, use a washer top wire, instead of a bottom wire, from which to hang the shade. The size of the shade is also easily adjusted. Just make sure the length of your paper equals that of the lampshade wire's circumference. Also, check that your grommets are spaced evenly around the shade.

Variation
To add some color to this shade, replace the hemp lacing with sea green gimp.

EXOTIC
PAPER SHADES

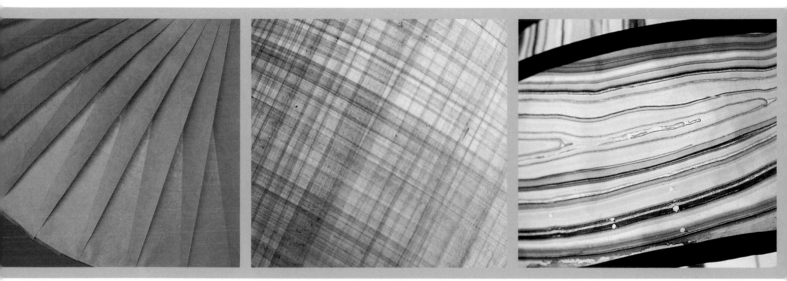

MUSICAL SCRIPT COOLIE

The square coolie is a perfect shape to complement an arts-and-crafts style lamp base. In this project, two papers are used to create an alternating pattern from side to side. Framing the sides with trim accentuates this play in patterns and lends this shade a certain distinction. This particular shade would work well in a study or near a music corner in your house. By simply changing the paper choice, be it in pattern or color, it can go in just about any room, including a bedroom.

Paper Choice

Vellum tends to pucker once the glue adhering it to the frame wires dries. To smooth any rippling or puckering before covering with the paper trapezoids, blow on it with hot air from a hair dryer. The heat will help pull the vellum taut.

Materials

- 1 25" x 38" (64 cm x 97 cm) sheet of medium weight translucent vellum

- 1 19" x 27" (48 cm x 69 cm) sheet of musical print paper

- 1 19" x 27" (48 cm x 69 cm) sheet of antique parchment

- 1 6" x 16" x 11" (15 cm x 41 cm x 28 cm) washer top square coolie frame

- 4 feet (1.2 m) of $\frac{1}{8}$" (.3 cm) wide black soutache trim

- 2 $\frac{1}{2}$ yards (2.2 m) of $\frac{3}{8}$" (1 cm) wide black grosgrain trim

- 4 feet (1.2 m) of $\frac{1}{8}$" (.3 cm) wide black grosgrain trim

- Double-stick Tape

- Basic Craft Supplies (see page 10)

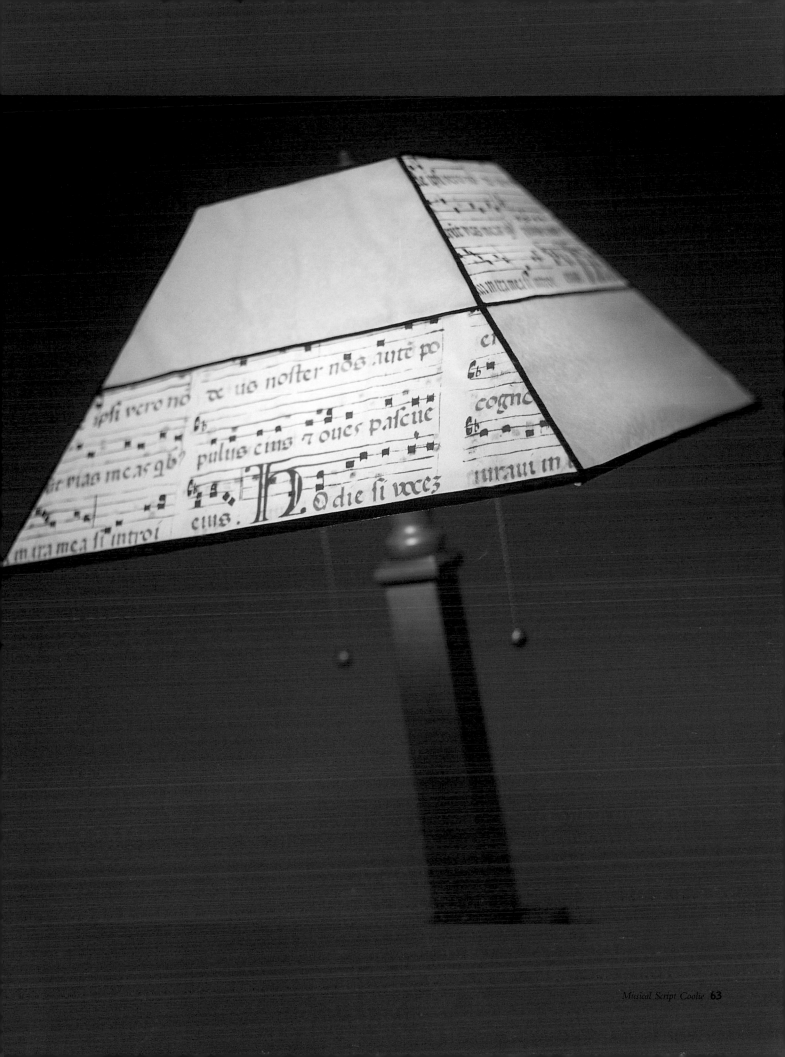

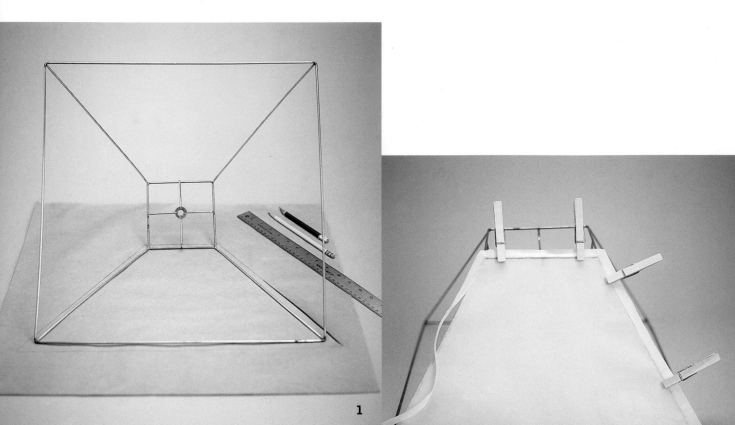

1

Step 1

Place the lampshade frame over a sheet of scrap paper and draw an outline, allowing for a ½" (1 cm) border. Cut the outline from the scrap paper and use as a template to cut out four vellum trapezoids.

Step 2

Trace a thin line of glue along the wires of one frame side. Spread evenly with your fingertip or a cotton swab. Lay the glue-coated frame side down on top of one of the vellum trapezoids making sure the vellum adheres to the frame smoothly. Trim off excess using a craft knife. You can use clothespins to hold in place while drying. Repeat with the other three sides.

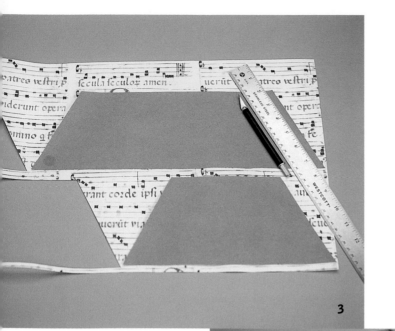

3

4

Step 3

Place the frame over a scrap piece of paper and draw an outline of one side as in step 1 but without any added border. Cut the outline and then fold in half horizontally. Cut along the fold line so that you have two smaller trapezoid templates—a top and a bottom. Using the top template cut two trapezoids from both the antique parchment and the scripted paper. Do the same with the bottom template. In total, you should have eight trapezoids.

Step 4

Outline the top half of a vellum panel with double-sided tape, matching the outline of the top trapezoid template, as shown. Carefully place one of the top parchment trapezoids over the tape to adhere to the shade. Similarly, outline the bottom half of the panel with double-sided tape. Adhere a bottom trapezoid from the scripted paper to the panel. Repeat around the shade making sure that the papers on the top and bottom panels alternate all the way around.

On each panel apply a strip of black soutache trim across the center so that it overlaps where the top and bottom trapezoid edges meet. Apply the ³/₈" (1 cm) trim in strips over the top and bottom wires of each panel. Run the ¹/₈" (.3 cm) black trim down the side ribs of each frame, tucking the ends under the top and bottom wires to finish.

Troubleshooting

Panel shades—square coolies, rectangular, hexagonal, etc.—are not always perfect in shape. That is, one side might be slightly off—a common error in the manufacturing process of lampshade frames. Since precision is required in covering the shade, hold one of the paper trapezoids up to make sure it matches up snug with the frame before adhering. Slight discrepancies can be fudged since the trim covers all the edges on this shade.

Variation

While there are papers sold with script and music notations, you could use actual sheet music or start with a blank sheet and make your own design.

STRIPED WHIMSY SHADE

Made with colorful strips of vellum dangling from silver rings, this shade evokes a smart playfulness that conjures up images of carousels, and general whimsy. This is a surprisingly simple shade to make and easily opens itself to variation, be it in the choice of color, pattern, shape of strips, or approach to attaching the strips to the lampshade frame. A clip-on lampshade makes attachment to the base quick and easy. This shade was made for a small base, however any size base can be used. To determine the proportionate size of strips you need for your base of choice, use cardboard or poster board to cut out and hang "test" pieces.

Materials

- eighteen Silver Pierced Earring Hoops, about 1 cm in diameter (or other thin-wired rings that can be threaded)

- eighteen silver eyelets

- one eyelet tool for sealing eyelets

- three 12" x 19" (30 cm x 48 cm) sheets of azure Chromatica translucent vellum (27 lb. weight)

- three 12" x 19" (30 cm x 48 cm) sheets of turquoise Chromatica translucent vellum (27 lb. weight)

- three 12" x 19" (30 cm x 48 cm) sheets of indigo Chromatica translucent vellum (27 lb. weight)

- one 7" (18 cm) clip-on single ring lampshade frame

- Multipurpose spray glue

- Clean, soft cloth

- Basic craft supplies (see page 10)

1

Step 1

Cover the work surface with paper bags or some other scrap paper that have been cut open so they lay flat to protect the counter from being coated with glue. Place one sheet of azure colored vellum on your work surface and lightly coat with spray glue all over. Take a second sheet of the azure vellum and adhere to the first, beginning in the corner to make an exact alignment. Repeat with a third sheet of the azure. Repeat again with the turquoise vellum and then the indigo vellum.

Step 2

Using the template on page 116, use a craft knife to cut six slats from each of the triple-layered papers so that you have a total of eighteen slats. Using the template as a guide, draw a circle $\frac{1}{2}$" (1 cm) from the top edge of each slat. Cut out the circle on the top of the slat to create a hole.

Troubleshooting

If you cannot find thin-wired earrings that are medium in size, you can always trim larger earrings with wire cutters. Then bend the loop accordingly to tighten the loop.

If your rings do not hold their latch easily, use needlenose pliers to squeeze the backing so that the wire cannot pull out. An alternative would be to apply glue.

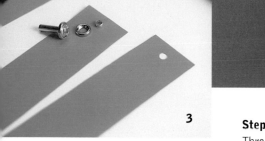

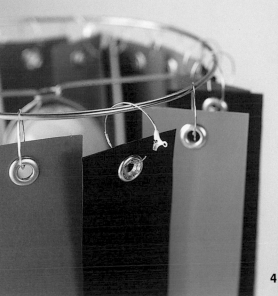

3

4

Step 3

Insert the deep half of the eyelet in the hole so that it is positioned on the front side of the slat. On the backside of the slat, fit the wider, shallow half of the eyelet onto the neck of the deep eyelet half. Place the wide end of the eyelet tool over the shallow half of the eyelet. On a firm, protected surface, use a hammer to strike the tool a few times so that the deep half of the eyelet rolls back over the shallow half.

Step 4

Thread a ring through the eyelet of a slat. Hang the ring on the lampshade frame. Repeat until all the slats are threaded and hanging. Space each ring about 1 ½" (4 cm) apart on the frame. Place the backing to the ring behind the slat so it is not readily visible.

Variation

To further the element of surprise with this shade, a sprinkling of confetti was trapped between two strips of lilac colored vellum. The strips were then hung from gold lanyard hooks instead of rings. This simple shade can be made with a wide variety of papers. It is important to use a fairly rigid paper that has some weight to it because the slats hang straight and uniformly. Or, if you have a particular paper in mind that is lightweight, use a heavy, stiff vellum or even cardboard for backing. This capricious style of shade particularly lends itself to vibrant colors.

PINK BOA SHADE

If only Barbie could wear this! It's hard to get any more playful than dressing a gathered pink paper shade with feather boa trim. While this diaphanous shade might find itself perfectly in place on a little girl's dresser, it might also find a perfect spot on a vanity or on display in the home of anyone with a flair for a little tongue-in-cheek kitsch. The machine-made paper used to create this shade is composed of hair-like rayon threads with gold and silver foil flecks dispersed randomly throughout. It is extremely lightweight and semi-transparent (more so when light is shined from behind it). Assembly of this shade requires elementary sewing skills. If you have never hand-basted before, you can learn here without worry. It gets no harder than being able to thread a needle.

Paper Choice

As if made from fabric, this shade gathers softly and loosely, so it's important to select a paper that is as supple and resilient as fabric. Rayon-based paper works ideally. There are also a number of soft lace papers that would work well for this shade. The paper you choose should be so soft that you could crumple it in your hand without its creasing or holding the shape when you release it.

Materials

- 1 sheet of 25" x 37" (64 cm x 94 cm) medium-weight translucent vellum
- 2 sheets of 21"x 31" (53 cm x 79 cm) burgundy lace rayon paper flecked with gold and silver
- 2 yards (1.9 m) of white feather boa, about 2 inches (5 cm) thick
- 1 round top washer lampshade wire 3 ½-inch (9 cm) diameter
- 1 round bottom lampshade wire 10-inch (84 cm) in diameter
- 1 needlepoint needle
- 1 sewing needle
- White sewing thread
- Basic craft supplies (see page 10)

Step 1

Using the template on page 118, make a cone shaped shade using the vellum paper. The top wire is meant to fit inside the vellum cone with the paper hanging over about $1/2$ inch. Likewise, the bottom wire will sit slightly inside the cone. Use a needlepoint needle to puncture two rows of holes along both the top and bottom edges of the cone to make stitch guides for step 4. Along the top edge, the puncture holes should be staggered about $1/2$ inch (1 cm) apart. Along the bottom edge, the holes should be staggered about one inch apart.

Step 2

Cut out both sheets of rayon paper using the template on page 119. Pin the two sheets together on top of one another. Thread a long strand of white thread through the sewing needle. Do not make a knot at the end of the thread. Baste stitch along the inside curved edge of the pink paper leaving at least six inches (15 cm) of string (not knotted) hanging from each end. The stitches should be about $3/4$-inch long (2 cm), and about $3/4$ inch (2 cm) in from the paper edge. Repeat basting along the outside curved edge.

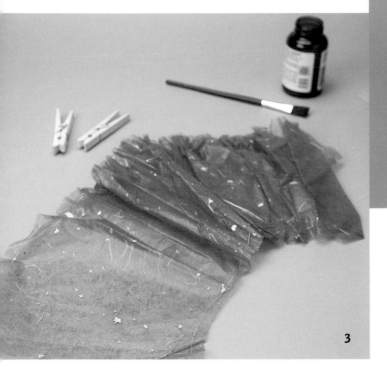

3

4

Step 3

To create gathers, hold onto one end of the thread used for basting the inside curve and push the paper towards the center edge of the curve. Repeat on the other side to complete the top gather. Then repeat on the outside curved edge to make the shades bottom gather. Use clothespins to wrap the gathered paper around the vellum shade, aligning seams accordingly. Adjust gathers as needed so that they balloon around the shade evenly. The seams of the gathered paper should overlap at least ½ inch (1 cm) and should hang loosely. Run a line of glue along the top and bottom edges of the vellum lampshade to adhere the gathered paper shade cover. Glue in between the clothespins. Once dry, remove the clips and finish gluing. Let dry.

Step 4

Clip away the excess basting thread. Beginning at the back seam of the shade, sew the feather boa to the top edge, using the punch holes as guides for zigzag stitching. Once the boa has completely wrapped around the top edge, clip it. Use the remaining boa to stitch to the bottom edge of the shade.

CRUSHED LEATHER LOUVRED SHADE

The simple technique of overlapping strips of paper puts a modern twist on the pleated shade (and absolves the crafter from the meticulous challenge involved with pleating). Because of the wide-brimmed shape of the shade, the strips of paper splay out at the bottom. This creates a pattern of shadows that tapers to a point at the shade base, like warm rays of sun bathing the lamp.

This shade is dramatically wide-brimmed and can take on a variety of base types, depending on the effect you wish to create. Here a tall, narrow base was used to create a neckiness to the ensemble. A stout, round ceramic base would work equally well.

The paper used here is manufactured to resemble crushed leather. Like so many artistic papers, this one takes on a whole new effect when placed in front of light. In this case, the texture of the paper—like that of soft, crushed leather—becomes accentuated.

This shade is composed of multiple, narrow slats of paper, so it is delicate. Be sure to place it where it is least likely to get bumped or snagged.

Paper Choice

There are a lot of lines and angles to this shade, so a simple, plain paper works best. When selecting the paper, hold it up to the light. It should be slightly translucent, ensuring that the shadows where the slats overlap will be pronounced when the lamp is lit.

Materials

- 2 sheets of 19" x 27" (48 cm x 53 cm) heavyweight translucent vellum

- 2 sheets of 21" x 31" (53 cm x 79 cm) amber "faux crushed leather" paper

- 1 washer top lampshade frame wire, 4" (10 cm) in diameter

- 1 bottom lampshade frame wire, 18" (46 cm) in diameter

- Basic craft supplies (see page 10)

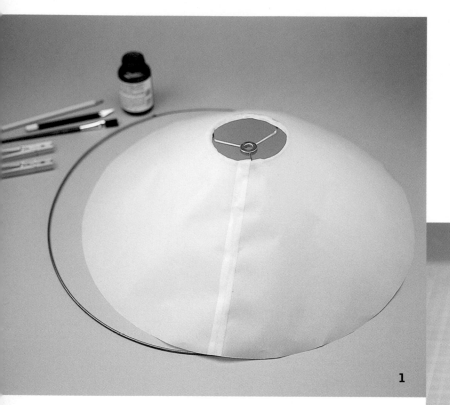

1

Step 1

Use the template on page 122 to cut the vellum sheets into two arcs. Glue one of the plain vellum arcs to the frame wires making a cone shape. Trim any paper that hangs beyond the wires. In accordance with the pattern of dotted lines on the template, lightly pencil in guidelines on the remaining unattached vellum arc. Lay the arc-penciled side facing up-on your work surface on top of a large sheet of scrap paper.

Step 2

Use a craft knife to cut the crushed leather paper into thirty-three slats, each 2" x 9 ½" (5 cm x 24 cm). At each end of the paper slats, mark a "v" shape at the halfway point.

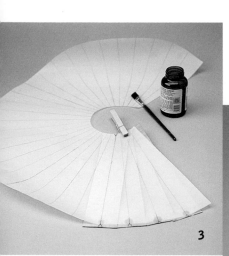

3

Step 3

At one far end of the vellum arc, slide a slat ("v" side up) under the arc and align the mid-points of the slat with the ends of the first penciled line on the arc. The slat should project slightly beyond the curved edges of the arc. Spread a small dab of glue or piece of double-stick tape near the center base of the slat to tack in place to the arc. Leave the top end unglued. Repeat, aligning and gluing all but two slats to the arc up to the last two lines. Do not glue the top ends of the slats in place.

4

Step 4

Carefully flip the slatted arc over and wrap it around the shade. Run a thin line of glue three-quarters of the way around the top edge of the vellum shade to adhere the top of the slatted arc to the shade. Do not run glue under the top edge of the first five slats. They need to remain open for the missing two slats to be inserted. Hold the top edge of the shade in place with clothespins if necessary while the glue dries. Insert the remaining two slats into position, the last of which will overlap more than average. Glue the two remaining slats and the first five in place at the top edge. Dot glue beneath the bottom corners of the slats to complete.

Troubleshooting

If the paper you choose is particularly thin or lightweight, you may wish to reinforce the paper slats. To do so, simply cut thirty-three slats, each 4" x 9 ½" (10 cm x 24 cm). Fold them in half lengthwise and position on the shade so that the folded edge is what sits on the outside.

Variation

You can vary the look of this shade by making a solid arc with a patterned paper of choice (that is, skip the steps of covering the shade with overlapping slats). Instead, stitch wooden skewers to the shade to create an umbrella-like feel.

CORK LAMPSHADE
with Faux Leather Stitching

Pressed cork paper is one of the most fascinating papers available—if just for the fact that it doesn't seem like paper at all! It has the cushioned feel of cork, the speckled markings of cork, and the warm wood-like face of cork. And this paper works great for shades. It is sturdy and decisive in its presence. However, pressed cork paper is not translucent, so do not choose this shade for a space where you really need light to splay out.

The available size of pressed cork paper—20" x 30" (51 cm x 76 cm)—dictates that two pieces are needed to wrap around the entire shade. Because of the variegated patterning of the cork, however, the double seams will go unnoticed.

Materials

- 1 strip of 9" x 33" (23 cm x 84 cm) craft paper

- 1 sheet of 20"x 30" (51 cm x 76 cm) pressed cork (cut into two 9" x 17" (23 cm x 43 cm) rectangles)

- 1 top lampshade wire, 10" (25 cm) (either clip-on or washer style) in diameter

- 1 bottom lampshade wire, 10" (25 cm) in diameter

- 4 yards (3.5 m) of brown leather-like cord

- Basic craft supplies (see page 10)

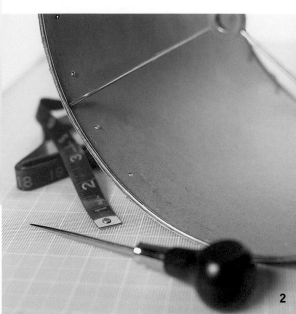

1

2

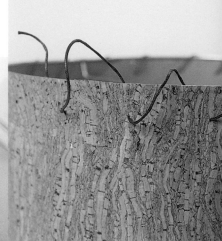

Step 1

Using the craft paper, follow step one on page 38 to make a drum-shaped shade 9" (23 cm) in. Run a line of glue almost halfway around the top edge of the drum shade. Adhere one sheet of the cork paper to the shade, leaving about an inch along one edge free (as shown). Repeat along half of the bottom edge-minus 1" (3 cm). Let dry. Run a line of glue around the remaining top edge of the drum shade. Adhere the second cork sheet, tucking one of its edges under the 1" (3 cm) long free edge of the first cork strip. This way, one end of each strip over-laps the other. Glue the bottom edge as well. Run glue or double-stick tape under the side seams to seal.

Step 2

Using an awl or other sharp pointed object, such as a needlepoint needle, puncture holes around the top and bottom edge of the shade. The holes should be positioned $5/8$" (1.5 cm) in from the wire edges and $1\ 5/8$" (4 cm) apart. The easiest way to measure around the shade is by using a flexible seamstress tape.

Step 3

Thread the leather-like cord through a hole coming from the front of the shade through to the back (leave enough slack to tie off ends). Pull the cord over the wire edge and thread again through the hole to the immediate left, again coming from the front. Repeat around the shade. You may find that the tip of the cord occasionally needs to be snipped at an angle with scissors to be able to thread the cord through with ease.

Variations

In addition to traditional ribbon trim, there are boundless options for adding a decorative finish to your paper shade. The following are just a handful of ideas using actual paper trims or common paper embellishments:

Raffia is a perfect partner to so many handmade papers. Here 6 strands are simply twisted together to trim along the edge of a mulberry paper.

Alternatively, run a single strand along the edge, looping the raffia at intervals for a soft, decorative touch.

Step 4
Once you have stitched around the entire shade, tie the string ends together in a knot on the inside of the shade.

Step 5
For a subtle decorative finish, between the first and last stitches overlap two small stitches to make an "X" shape to complete.

Troubleshooting

- *When working with pressed cork paper, it is important that the grain runs vertically on the shade. If you bend the cork so that the grain wraps around the shade, the cork will split. If you are uncertain how the grain runs on your paper, try rolling a test swatch. It will naturally roll parallel with the grain. It will resist and the cork will crackle if rolled perpendicular to the grain.*

- *Use the backside of the paper, which is white, to mark measurements. Pencil marks easily get lost in the maze of texture and speckling on the cork side.*

Tiny paper flowers are gathered side-by-side to make an ornate, three-dimensional trim. An awl was used to puncture holes along the paper edge to thread the wire stems of these flowers through to the back side of the paper.

For a more organic look, fossilized citrus leaves were overlapped and held down with a coordinating bark-colored paper ribbon.

Soft unryu paper in peach was folded to create a delicate pleated trim with orange raffia stitching as an accent.

A strip of Italian spiral-patterned paper adds interest to an otherwise plain paper backdrop. Cut paper into a narrow strip and fold in half with diamond cutouts falling at intervals along the fold.

PAPYRUS SHADE LAMP

Papyrus paper's woven quality is quite beautiful when light shines through with a warm, soft glow. Pair the papyrus shade with a quirky base, perhaps an attic treasure or flea market find: vases and bottles can easily be converted with a simple lamp kit. Once you've assembled one lamp, you'll see how easy it is to make one from almost anything hollow, whether a figurine, teapot, or pitcher.

Materials

- Vellum lining paper (size according to base or use the template)

- Large sheet of papyrus

- Template on page 110

- One package of $\frac{1}{4}$-inch (.5 cm) double fold bias binding, off-white

- Fabric glue

- Double-sided adhesive tape

- Basic Craft Supplies (see page 10)

- Washer top lampshade wire

- Bottom lampshade wire

Step 1

Cut the lining paper and papyrus to size using the template on page 110. Glue the lining paper arc around the top wire of the shade.

Step 2

Once the arc is attached to the top wire, remove every other clothespin and let dry. Prop the shade upside down (on the end tips of the clothespins) so that it does not warp or shift while drying.

Step 3

Join and adhere the sides of the paper arc, overlapping the paper about $\frac{1}{2}$" (1 cm), to form a seam. Use double-sided adhesive tape.

Step 4

Set the shade upside down, and glue the bottom wire to the bottom of the shade.

Tip: Vellum and papyrus tend to pucker as the glue dries. To smooth any rippling or puckering where the vellum has been glued to the frame wires, blow on it with hot air from a hairdryer. The heat will help to pull the paper taut.

Step 5

Apply double-sided tape or a line of glue around the top and bottom edges of the shade, as well as along the seam. Wrap the papyrus paper arc created in step 1 around the shade starting at the seam. Cut fabric trim to size for the top and bottom of the shade. Using fabric glue, secure the trim to the edges of the shade, inside and out (see Trimming Lampshades on p. 24).

DOUBLE-DECKER MARBLED LAMPSHADE

Here two shades, topped one on the other, make one shade—and a surprisingly different one at that. To add to the fun, the shades are made with Thai hand-marbled paper that makes this shade all the more exotic.

There is nothing tricky about crafting this shade. You simply make a basic drum-shaped shade, albeit much shorter and wider than an average shade, in order to create a more dramatic effect. Then you prop a smaller shade on top. No unusual hardware is required to suspend two shades over one base. You simply need to line the top shade with a heavyweight vellum or parchment so that it can stand up on its own on top of the spokes of the bottom shade.

One distinctive touch with this shade is that two layers of trim are applied. The first is applied in a traditional manner to wrap over the shade and its structural wires. The second is laid flat around the shade edge so that it creates a thick band with a crisp edge along the top and bottom edges of the shade.

This shade will work equally well with less dramatic papers. You can use the same paper for each shade level or try mixing and matching patterns or varying colors. Just about anything goes.

Materials

- 1 large sheet 25"x36" (64 cm x 91 cm) of heavyweight translucent parchment or vellum for shade lining

- 1 large sheet 25"x36" (64 cm x 91 cm) of Thai marbled paper

- 16" (41 cm) washer top lampshade wire

- 16" (41 cm) bottom lampshade wire

- 12" (30 cm) washer top lampshade wire

- 12" (30 cm) bottom lampshade wire

- 10 $\frac{1}{2}$ yards (9.6 m) of black $\frac{5}{8}$" (1.5 cm) wide grosgrain trim

- Basic craft supplies (see page 10)

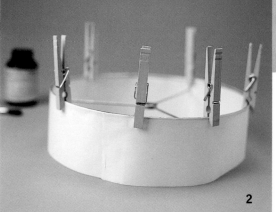

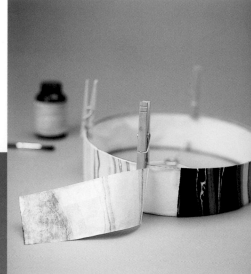

Step 1

Using a craft knife, cut the paper for the shade lining into two rectangles: one measuring 8" x 52" (20 cm x 132 cm) and the other 3" x 39" (8 cm x 99 cm). Do the same with the marbled paper. It is unlikely you will find either paper in 52" (132 cm) lengths. To remedy, make the large rectangle with two pieces measuring 8" x 26 ¼" (20 cm x 26.5 cm). Adhere with glue or double-stick tape along one short edge by overlapping ½" (1 cm). For the marbled paper, try to overlap with pieces that have similar edges so as not to disrupt the pattern too dramatically, as shown here.

Step 2

Glue a long edge of the 8" x 52" (20 cm x 132 cm) sheet of to the 16" (41 cm) top wire. Clip with clothespins while the glue dries. Repeat the process with the 3" x 39" (8 cm x 99 cm) lining and the 12" (30 cm) top wire. Once the glue has dried, glue the bottom edges of each lining to the corresponding bottom wires.

Step 3

Cover large drum and small drums with marbled paper using double-stick adhesive tape or glue. If gluing, hold in place with clothespins until dry.

4

Step 4

Glue trim along the top and bottom edges of each drum, folding over the edges to cover frame wires inside the shade. Hold in place to dry with clothespins. Once dry, apply a second layer of trim around the outside top and bottom edges of both shades so that the trim edges fall flush with, rather than fold over, the edges of the shades. Use double-stick tape or glue. If using glue, hold trim in place with clothespins to dry.

5

Step 5

Secure the large drum to the lamp base, securing in place with a finial. Set the small drum on top, propping it on the spokes of the top wire of the large drum.

Troubleshooting

• *This project uses quite a lot of trim. If you're shy on trim, cut a supple paper into ⁵/₈" (1.5 cm) wide long strips and apply as the under layer of trim that wraps inside and over the top and bottom frame wires.*

• *When applying the second layer of trim to the shade, set the shade at eye level on the lamp to achieve accuracy. Hold in place with the finial and gently spin the shade as you work around it.*

Variation

If a double-decker shade is not daring enough, why not push the limit and make a triple-decker? For this shade, the third tier was made with 8" (20 cm) diameter frame wires.

VOTIVES AND NIGHT-LIGHTS

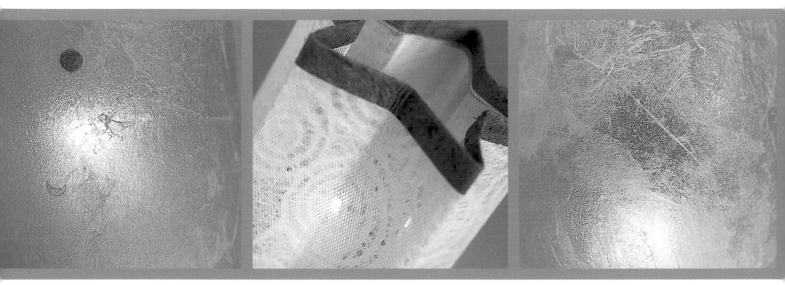

DRAGONFLY NIGHT-LIGHT

A night-light is one of the few lights in a home that almost always shines alone and in the pitch dark of the night. So why not make it a light that is pleasing to the eye—especially to the weary eye.

This particular shade is shaped like a sconce to curve well around the night-light bulb. It is also large enough to cover a standard outlet frame. For this project, be sure to pair the shade with a night-light fixture that takes a cold-burning bulb. You can find this kind of night-light in a hardware or general housewares store.

Night-lights are particularly conducive to construction with sculpted wire because they are small and do not need a heavy, rigid wire for support. You might wish to buy extra wire, however. These shades can be so inspiring to sculpt with that you might just end up making more than one.

Materials

- 1 sheet of 9 $\frac{1}{2}$" x 11" (24 cm x 28 cm) vellum with gold dragonfly pattern

- 18-gauge pearlized gold wire cut into the following lengths: 26" (66 cm), 9" (23 cm), and 7 $\frac{1}{2}$" (19 cm)

- 24-gauge pearlized wire cut into the following length: 18" (46 cm)

- 1-inch (3 cm) wide gold sparkle abaca ribbon or other trim, cut into the following lengths: 9" cm) and 7" (18 cm)

- Standard and needle-nose pliers

- Wire cutters

- 28 oz. (.8 liters) aluminum can or 4" (10 cm) diameter aluminum can

- 3 $\frac{1}{2}$" (9 cm) diameter can

- 1 night-light with a cold-burning bulb

- Double-sided tape

- 1 gold, finish nail

- Basic craft supplies (see page 10)

1

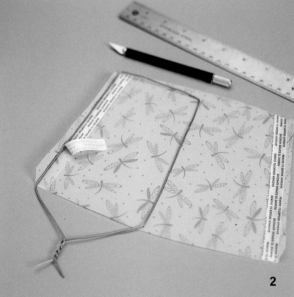

2

Step 1

Using a square edge such as the corner of a table, bend the 26" (66 cm) wire to conform to the template shape on page 120. With the pliers, grip the wires just below the point at which they intersect, making an "x." Hold the wire tips together with the needle-nose pliers and twist until they are wrapped around one another.

Step 2

Cut the shade cover from the vellum paper using the template on page 121. Using the back-side of a craft knife, score the backside of the paper $\frac{1}{2}$" (3 cm) in from the two straight sides. Place a strip of the double-sided adhesive tape along the inside edges of the scored lines. Position the wire frame so that the long straight edges of the frame sit on the paper's scored lines. Fold the paper over the wires to adhere to the tape and lock in the wires.

Step 3

Bend the 18-gauge 9" (23 cm) wire halfway around the 28 oz. (.8 liters) can to create a curve. Insert the curved wire inside the shade so that it sits $\frac{3}{8}$" (1 cm) below the top curved edge. Glue to the inside of the shade using clothes pins to hold the wire in place as the glue dries. Using the needle-nose pliers, wrap the wire tips around to the front sides of the shade. Wrap the 7 $\frac{1}{2}$" (19 cm) wire halfway around the smaller aluminum can. Adhere to the bottom curved edge of the shade using the same method as for the top wire.

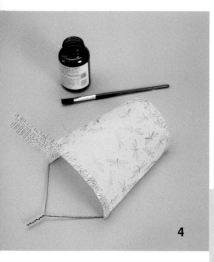

4

Step 4

Using glue, adhere the 7" (18 cm) gold trim to the bottom rounded edge of the shade so that ¹/₂" (3 cm) of the trim hangs over the outside edge. Repeat with the 9" (23 cm) trim on the top rounded edge.

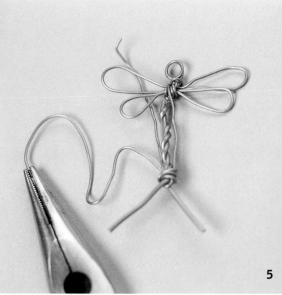

5

Step 5

Sculpt a design of choice with the 18-gauge wire and attach it by lassoing it to the frames twisted top wires. Position the finished shade over the plugged-in night-light, using a finish nail to hold the shade in place.

Troubleshooting

While you can find 18-gauge and 24-gauge wire in hardware stores, they are not necessarily designed for crafting. It can be particularly difficult to smooth out any kinks. The same gauge wire found in craft stores is designed for sculpting, so it is much more malleable. To get clean, round shapes, use a pencil or other round object around which to wrap the wire. To smooth out kinks, firmly press the wire against a pen or other round object with your thumb and pull the wire through. Repeat if necessary.

Variation

For this project, you can sculpt just about any design you would like to lash to the nightlight's wire frame. Perhaps you would like to coordinate it with wallpaper or a room theme, such as leaves. Just make sure the wire-sculpted design includes a centrally located loop to hang the shade by.

RIPPLED FOIL VOTIVE

The natural beauty of unique papers can be used not only to diffuse light but also to reflect it. Foil papers prove ideal for this effect and come in a variety of metal tones and even textures.

A hammered copper paper was used in this project for its unique textural component and the added warmth copper contributes to the candlelight. A dark paper with copper marbling was selected for backing to give the votive added structure and a midnight feel.

The basic shape of the votive is similar to that of an electric drip coffee filter and is very simply made by gently molding the paper around a round, tapered object. The grass wreath surrounding the base finishes the presentation, while displaying your work on a candle stand pronounces the delivery.

Materials

- 1 sheet of embossed foil paper cut into a 9" x 9" (23 cm x 23 cm)

- 1 sheet of black construction paper with metallic marbling or other sturdy weight paper cut into a 9" x 9" (23 cm x 23 cm)

- Small bunch of dried wild grass (available at craft stores)

- 9 strands of 5" (13 cm) copper or natural raffia

- 1 medium size permanent marker (or object of similar shape and size)

- 1 square candle stand, 5"x5" (13 cm x 13 cm)

- 1 drip-proof candle, 3" tall x 2" wide (8 cm tall x 5 cm wide)

- 2 ½" (6 cm) round glass candle plate

Step 1

Glue the backsides of the black marbled paper and foil paper together. Cut out an 8 ¹/₂" (22 cm) diameter circle from the glued papers. Using a pencil, lightly draw a 2 ¹/₂" (6 cm) circle in the center of the paper circle on the foil side (see dotted line on template for guide). Place the marker tip (cap on) at the edge of the inner circle and gently mold outer circle around the marker. At the edge of the inner circle the paper should just barely mold around the marker tip; do not crease it. The curves should be soft and less pronounced towards the center of the disc.

Step 2

Place the marker on the back-side (black paper side) of the disc about 1" (3 cm) to the right of where it was previously positioned. As in step 1, mold the paper around the marker to create another, opposing, curve. Repeat around the disc to create a rippled effect.

4

Troubleshooting

Foil papers are not so forgiving when you smudge even the least bit of glue on them. To minimize the risk of getting any glue on the paper, place the foil face down on a clean surface and glue the black paper on top of it (instead of vice versa). If there is any glue on your hands, it will smudge on the black paper, where it is less likely to show. To be safe, always keep a damp cloth nearby to keep your hands clean while applying glue and handling papers.

3

Step 4

Once you've made a 16" (41 cm) chain, wrap it into a circular shape, lashing the top 1" (3 cm) of the first shock of grass with the base of the last to form a wreath with a 3 ½" (9 cm) diameter. Trim off ends of the raffia ties and center the wreath on the candle stand. Position the rippled foil "basket" inside the wreath and place the glass candle plate inside the votive. Set the candle on top of the plate.

Step 3

Make a chain of dried grass. To make the chain, overlap one shock of dried grass about 1" (3 cm) below the tip of the first. Using a strand of raffia, tie the shocks of grass together at one-inch intervals. Trim off any woody stems as you go along.

Variation

In addition to foil papers, there are a number of other papers to choose from that have reflective properties, such as this "opalescent" paper. Gold leaf is another excellent alternative if you are adept at working with it.

Rippled Foil Votive **97**

STARLIGHT HANGING LAMPSHADE

Perhaps the most ethereal and yet tactile of papers are Japanese lace papers. Their intricate webs of threading suggest a delicacy unlike any other. Yet these papers can be crumpled up and tugged upon and still maintain structural integrity. The "see-through" nature of lace papers works particularly well with this hanging shade, in which miniature lights twinkle through the paper's open weave. Consider this more a decorative "night-light" than a functional source of illumination.

Lace papers do not adhere well with glue to shade wires, particularly when there is no backing to the shade, as is the case for this shade. For this reason, the paper in this project is treated like a fabric and actually stitched to the wires.

Materials

- 1 washer top lampshade wire, 10" (25 cm) in diameter

- 1 bottom lampshade wire, 10" (25 cm) in diameter

- 1 clip shade adapter

- Twist ties

- 1 strand of small white Christmas tree lights

- 1 large sheet of steel blue Japanese lace paper, cut into a 32" x 20" (81 cm x 51 cm) rectangle

- Raffia

- Double-stick tape

- Sewing Needle

- Steel-blue thread

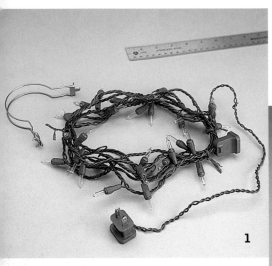

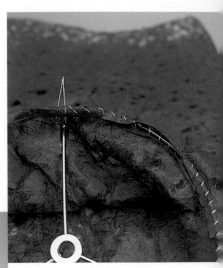

Step 1

Wrap the strand of lights into 8" (20 cm) length loops. Use a twist tie to pull together the strands at one end of the loop. At the other end, sling a clip shade adapter underneath.

1

Step 2

Use double-stick tape to adhere the first 10" (25 cm) of the 20" (51 cm) sides of the rectangle to form a cylinder shape. Leave the remaining 10" (25 cm) unattached for the time being.

2

Step 3

Fold in by ½" (1 cm) the top edge of the cylinder. Fold again by ¼" (.5 cm) over the top frame wire and whipstitch to attach, here shown in a contrasting thread to better exemplify. Also, whipstitch the bottom lampshade wire to the paper cylinder so that it sits 10" (25 cm) below the top wire.

Tip: To make sure the bottom wire falls evenly 10" (25 cm) below the top wire, you may find yourself constantly keeping measure. One short-cut is to use a fabric pencil to mark the paper 10 ¾" (27 cm) below the top edge before forming the cylinder in step 2. (The additional ¾" [2 cm] takes into account the folding in step 3.)

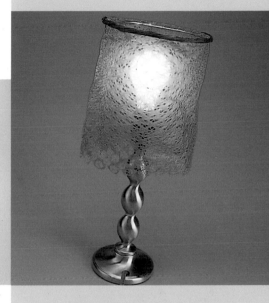

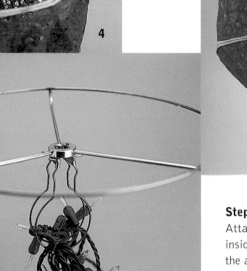

Troubleshooting

This shade has little or no rigidity. So construct as much of the shade as possible before inserting the strand of lights; otherwise, you will encounter some awkward handling. Finally, make sure your strand of lights is the type that does not heat up. As with any shade, keep the paper out of direct contact with any bulbs.

4

5

6

Step 4
Tie strands of raffia to the three spokes in the top wire and knot together at the ends to form a loop from which you can hang the shade. Glue the raffia around the shade where the top and bottom wires are positioned.

Step 5
Attach the strand of lights inside the shade by clipping the adapter to the washer top wire, seen here with the shade removed to better illustrate how the adapter attaches.

Step 6
Pull the loose bottom 10" (25 cm) of the shade together and wrap numerous times with raffia to gather, tying to hold in place.

Variation

As seen here, you can make this shade with an open bottom. It can be used as a hanging shade or as one set on top of a lamp base. The bottom edges of the shade shown here were clipped to create a scalloped effect.

LEAF AND PAPER HURRICANE

Press leaves and flowers to keep a bit of nature all year round. The pretty shapes of botanicals look best combined with the uneven texture of handmade papers—just make sure to test the translucency of the paper by holding it up the light. This hurricane, which assembles in less than an hour, can be made to reflect the seasons: use rose petals for a warm weather look, fall leaves at the change of the season, and bits of evergreen for a frosty, wintery glow. Experiment by using bits of torn paper, rather than a whole piece, to cover the container with a textured collage.

Materials

- Tall clear container, such as a vase or a hurricane shade
- A handful of pressed leaves or flowers
- One sheet of Japanese handmade paper
- Découpage glue
- Foam applicator brush
- Basic Craft Supplies (see page 10)

Step 1

Trace the shape of the container by wrapping the paper around it, and marking the top and bottom edges of the container. Unwrap the container, and add $\frac{1}{4}$" (.5 cm) to the length for the seam. Next, tear the paper by laying a ruler along the pencil line and gently pulling the paper toward you. The irregular edges will produce a softer look and will help disguise the seam.

Step 2

Clean and dry the container. Using the foam applicator, apply a thin, even coat of glue on the vase where you will place the leaves or flowers. Arrange botanicals as desired, and gently smooth the leaves outward from the stem with the foam applicator. Be sure there are no wrinkles or air bubbles in the leaves or petals. For brittle or thick foliage, gently coat the back with glue first, which will make it more pliable.

Step 3

Gently apply a thin, even coat of glue to the entire container, including the leaves or flowers. Position one edge of the paper on the container where you want the seam to be and begin wrapping it on smoothly and slowly. Smooth out wrinkles and bubbles as you go along. Finally, apply another thin, even coat of glue over the paper and let it dry overnight before using.

Tip: It is easy to dry and press your own leaves in a heavy book: simply place between sheets of waxed paper and weight with the book for a week or two. Many craft stores offer flower presses and already dried flowers and leaves, as well. For easier lighting and the best effect, choose a candle that is about half as tall as the container

CUTOUT TEA LIGHTS

There is elegance in simplicity. These basic tea lights embody that. Here, a cutout of a stylized tree in a straight lined design provides the only decorative element. With cutout patterns, straightforward design is often the best. Create your own or refer to the templates on page 117. As with any paper votive, it is imperative for safety's sake that the candle is encased in a glass holder.

Materials

- 11" x 14" (28 cm x 36 cm) card stock or other heavyweight paper
- 1 small piece of white vellum
- Double-stick tape
- Craft knife

Step 1

Determine the height and width you want the shade to be. Here, the shade is 8 $\frac{1}{2}$" (22 cm) tall and 3" (8 cm) wide. To calculate the size, measure the diameter of the glass candleholder and add at least $\frac{1}{2}$" (1 cm) to get the width of each side of the shade. (This allows the minimum $\frac{1}{4}$" (.5 cm) breathing room on all sides of the holder.) Multiply the width times four; then add an additional $\frac{1}{4}$" (.5 cm) to create a flap for sealing the shade. For the shade here, an 8 $\frac{1}{2}$" x 12 $\frac{1}{4}$" (22 cm x 12.5 cm) rectangle was cut from the card stock.

Step 2

With a craft knife, score the rectangle into four equal panels leaving $\frac{1}{4}$" (.5 cm) strip at the end. For this project, the paper was scored to make four panels, 8 $\frac{1}{2}$" x 3" (22 cm x 8 cm) with the fifth panel measuring 8 $\frac{1}{2}$" x $\frac{1}{4}$" (22 cm x .5

cm) at a far end). Then, trace the pattern on page 117 on each panel and cut along the lines.

Step 3

Back each cutout with a piece of vellum using double-stick tape or a glue stick. On the front, glue a $\frac{1}{4}$" (.5 cm) border of a different colored paper around the design to "frame" it. Fold along the scored lines, and adhere the $\frac{1}{4}$" (.5 cm) flap to the inside of the shade to complete.

Variation

For a quick set of tea lights, cut a square out of each panel to frame a piece of printed, translucent paper such as the sea shell vellum seen here (above, right).

CUT AND PIERCED PARTY SHADES

The flicker of candlelight dancing through cutout and pierced designs on a paper votive will add party enchantment as the centerpiece to a dinner table or as a background accent in a room. To pierce paper, use an awl (a craft tool specifically used for piercing) or improvise with needles sewing, darning, knitting—or even some nails. The paper should have enough structure to permit a clean puncture. Black, fibrous papers with more rigid paper to allow a clean piercing. Setting the paper on a surface that yields to the point of the awl or other sharp object, such as an old towel, a blanket, or, with a small project, a few layers of thick paper towel.

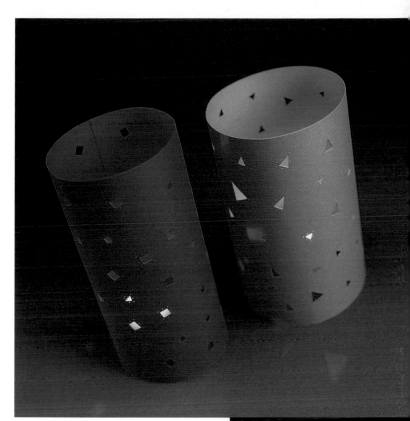

Materials

- 1 sheet of heavyweight red or orange paper (see step 1 for specifics on dimensions)

- Double-sided adhesive tape

- Glass encased votive candle

- Awl (see above for alternative tools)

- Old blanket or towel

- Basic craft supplies (see page 10)

Step 1
From the red or orange paper, cut out a rectangle that measures the same height as the candle-holder and 2" (5 cm) longer than the candle-holder's circumference.

Step 2
Using a craft knife, cut out $1/4$" to $1/2$" (.5 cm to 1 cm) squares or triangles from the paper. Do this freehand or make a cardboard template.

Step 3
With an awl or similar pointed tool, pierce holes at each corner of the squares and triangles. Also pierce a hole centered along each side.

Step 4
Finally, use a strip of $1/2$" (1 cm) wide double-stick tape to close the rectangle into a cylindrical shape; overlap each edge exactly $1/2$" (1 cm) for a complete seal and a neat finish.

Variation

Use hand punches to create a design like the one seen here, which uses $1/8$" (.3 cm) and $1/4$ inch (.5 cm) circles. Since hand punches will only reach about an inch or two (3 cm to 5 cm), $3/4$" wide (2 cm) strips of paper were punched and layered on vellum (above, right).

FOLDED STAR PAPER VOTIVE

Here, celestial, spiral lace paper is girded with wire mesh to fold into a star-shaped candle votive. The trickiest element to this simple shade project is working with the wire mesh. It's prickly, so wear protective gloves. It also can be brittle and easily broken, so you cannot make sharp creases when folding it into the star pattern. To avoid these problems, cut out the paper-covered wire mesh slightly longer than might be needed to allow room for error. Simply trim the excess with wire cutters or old shears.

Materials

- Dark blue paper
- Spiral lace paper
- Fine wire craft mesh
- Spray adhesive
- Work gloves
- Wire cutter or old scissors

Step 1

Cut a 7 ½" x 24" (19 cm x 61 cm) rectangle of wire mesh, using a wire cutter or old scissors. Wear work gloves.

Step 2

Cut a piece of spiral lace paper the same size as the mesh. Cut two strips of blue paper, 1" x 24" (3 cm x 61 cm), for the top and bottom border. Using spray adhesive, affix the borders to the top and bottom of the spiral paper. Next, affix the paper to the mesh with the spray adhesive. Be sure to protect your work surface with newspaper or scrap paper.

Step 3

Fold ½" (1 cm) of the top and bottom edges of the paper-coated wire to the back (see headnote). Fold one of the side edges ¼" (.5 cm) to the back. Measure 2" (5 cm) in from the crease of the folded side edge and fold the mesh in the opposite direction. Continue folding, alternating the direction each time for an accordion fold. Gently fold ten times. The tenth fold should be only ½" (1 cm) wide, so you may need to trim any excess. Glue this flap to the inside of the opposite edge to create and close the star.

Variation

Use a solid piece of color-blended translucent paper for an instant design, like the "sunrise" unryu rice paper used here. To make a triangular shape, fold the mesh three times, with the last fold being ½" (1 cm). Close the triangle as described in Step 3 above.

TISSUE PAPER HURRICANE

If you don't have an old glass hurricane shade hanging

around in your basement or storage closet, you can certainly find one second hand. Making

this shade does not require skill with a craft knife. All you have to do is tear the paper into

pieces. The torn edges blend together visually for a soft look. And a third color is naturally

introduced when pieces of paper made from two different colors overlap, as seen here. Because

it is very difficult to handle wet tissue paper, be sure to apply glue to the hurricane shade,

not to the paper. In the variation, since the tissue, when dry, is very translucent, the foil glitter

still sparkles even when covered.

Materials

- 1 glass hurricane shade
- Collage glue (clear and fast drying)
- 2 sheets of tissue paper in two or more colors (or any other sheer, transparent papers)
- Foam brush

Step 1
Tear tissue paper into large and medium-sized pieces.

Step 2
Apply glue with a foam brush to a small area of the hurricane shade.

Step 3
Apply pieces of the tissue over the glue, and gently smooth out with your fingers. Continue applying glue and adding tissue to cover the vase, overlapping the edges to blend the colors.

Variation
Completely cover a shade with very large pieces of blue tissue and let dry. Buy confetti, or make some using decorative hand punches. Gold and silver foil paper punched with crescent, star, and circle hand punches were used for the luminary seen here. Apply a thin layer of glue to a small area of the shade and sprinkle with confetti. Continue around the shade, working in small sections. Use a toothpick to adjust any of the confetti. Apply another layer of large pieces of tissue over the confetti (above, right).

TEMPLATES

For those projects in the book that require templates, the following pages contain actual-size or reduced-sized versions. Each page containing a template will indicate what percent you need to increase it on a photocopy machine to bring it to its full size.

When making the most basic lampshade—the round empire shade—it is particularly crucial that you are working with a precise template. The template shape for an empire shade is an arc form. The mathematics to creating your own arc can be tricky. Additionally, it requires drafting tools that the average crafter does not have on hand. It is advisable to have an arc template drafted for you. Many sources for lampshade fixtures supply just this service and do so inexpensively. To order a drafted arc, you will need the diameter of the top of the shade and the base of the shade. You will also need the length of the shade's side. Of course, if you are restoring an existing lampshade, your other option is to wrap scrap or tracing paper around the shade and draw its outline to replicate the size of the arc you need.

THE BASIC SHADE

525%

BASIC BOX SHADE

352%

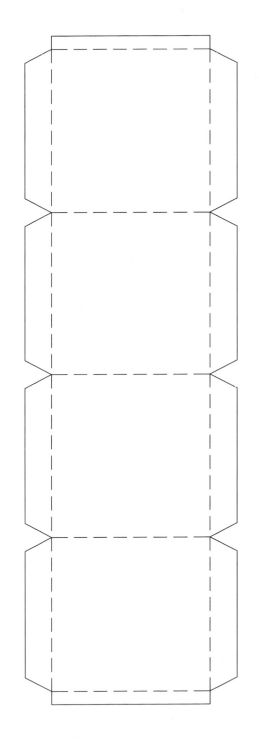

PAPER TWIST CONE

342%

TEMPLATE 1

COFFEE-DYED LAMPSHADE

with copper lashing

248%

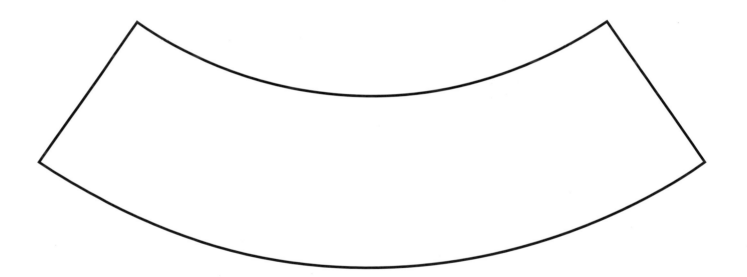

HEXAGONAL SCONCE SHADE

100% (actual size)

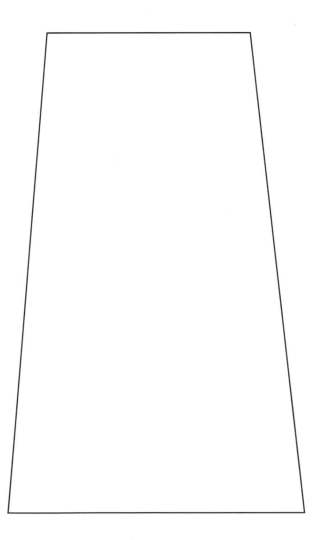

STRIPED WHIMSY SHADE

139%

CUTOUT TEA LIGHTS

148%

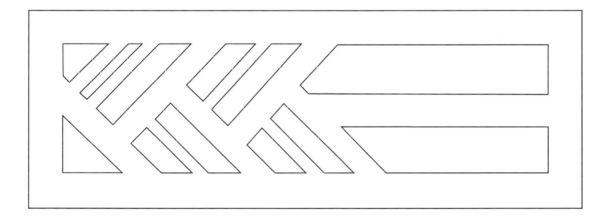

PINK BOA

410%

TEMPLATE 1

450%

TEMPLATE 2

DRAGONFLY NIGHT-LIGHT

175%

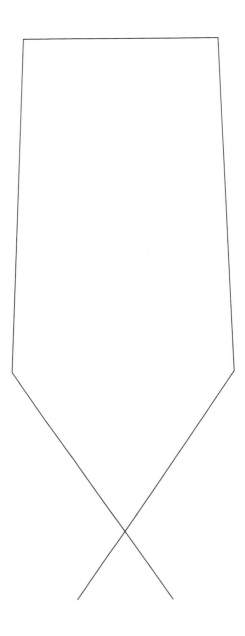

TEMPLATE 1

170%

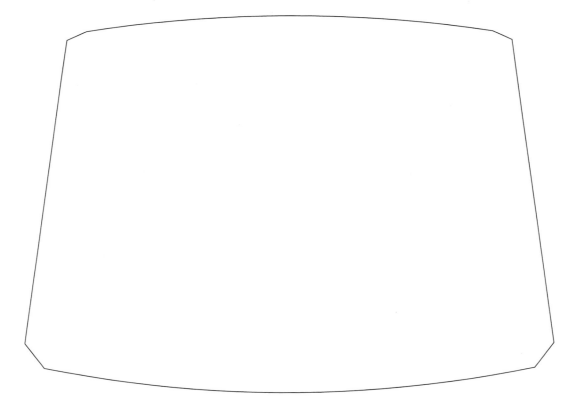

TEMPLATE 2

CRUSHED LEATHER LOUVRED SHADE

250%

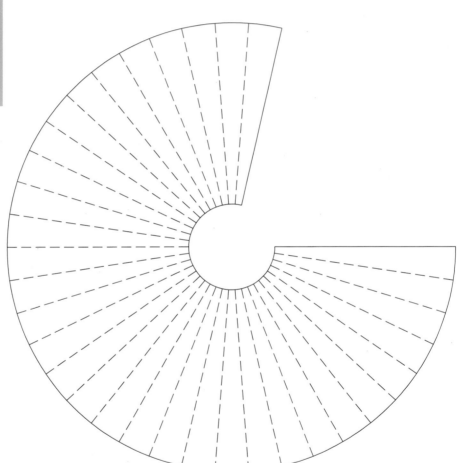

RESOURCES

A.C. Moore
500 University Court
Blackwood, NJ 08012
(856) 228-6700
See www.acmoore.com for
store locations
Art and craft supplies

Craftopia.com, Inc.
1336 Enterprise Drive
West Chester, PA 19380
1-800-373-0343
www.craftopia.com
Papers, art and craft supplies

Dick Blick Art Materials
P.O. Box 1267
Galesburg, IL 61402-1267
800-447-8192
www.dickblick.com
Papers, art and craft supplies
Catalog available

Fascinating Folds
P.O. Box 10070
Glendale, AZ 85318
800-968-2418
www.fascinating-folds.com
Wide selection of papers,
paper supplies, and paper
embellishments
Catalog available

Kate's Paperie
561 Broadway
New York, NY 10012
212-941-9816
Extensive selection of papers
and paper-related supplies
Will ship papers by mail order

Lamp Specialties
Box 240
Westville, NJ 08093-0240
856-931-1283
Lamp and shade parts, kits,
craft supplies
Catalog available

Loose Ends
P.O. Box 20310
Salem, OR 97307-0310
503-393-2348
www.4loosends.com
Craft supplies, natural fiber
papers
Catalog available

Mainely Shades
100 Gray Road
Falmouth, ME 04105
800-624-6359
www.mainelyshades.com
Lampshade wires and parts,
pre-drafted arc templates,
lamp making supplies
Catalog available

Michaels
850 North Lake Dr.
Suite 500
Coppell, TX 75028
800-642-4235
See www.michaels.com for
store locations
Art and craft supplies

The Paper Crane
280 Cabot Street
Beverly, MA 01915
978-927-3131
Wide selection of papers,
paper supplies, and paper
embellishments

Paper Source
1810 Massachusetts Avenue
Cambridge, MA 02140
617-497-10777
Extensive selection of papers
and paper-related supplies
Will ship papers by mail order

Pearl Paint
308 Canal Street
New York, NY 10013-2572
800-451-PEARL
Art and craft supplies
Catalog available

Rugg Road
105 Charles Street
Boston, MA
617-742-0002
Extensive selection of papers
and paper-related supplies
Will ship papers by mail order

Shades of the Past
P.O. Box 11
Tomkins Cove, NY 10986
888-786-3244
http://hometown.aol.com/
sotpast/supplies.htm
Lampshade parts and supplies

Maryellen Driscoll lives on a small working farm at the foot of the Adirondack Mountains. A tireless crafter, writer, gardener, and cook, Driscoll enjoys the challenges and rewards of making things by hand. A former editor at *Cook's Illustrated* magazine, she is a contributing author to *Brilliant Food Tips and Cooking Tricks* (Rodale, 2001) and has written for a number of national magazines and major newspapers.

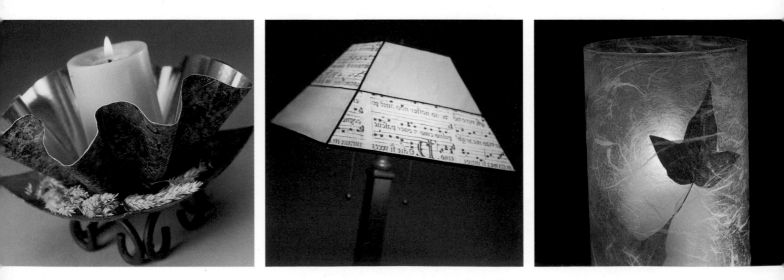